Epicure's
Delectable Desserts of the World

Epicure's

Delectable Desserts of the World

Asha Khatau

Popular Prakashan

POPULAR PRAKASHAN PVT. LTD.
35-C, Pt. Madan Mohan Malaviya Marg
Popular Press Building,Tardeo,
Mumbai 400 034
Shop online at www.popularprakashan.com

First Published 2005

ISBN- 81-7991-228-0
(3976)

Photography by Mangesh Parab
Cover Design by Siddharth Ganguly

Typeset & Designed
by Vans Information Ltd.
35-C, Pt. Madan Mohan Malaviya Marg
Tardeo, Mumbai 400 034.

Printed in India by
New Model Impex Pvt. Ltd.
Jagjivan Vidya Bhavan, Link Road
New Delhi 110055

Published by Ramdas Bhatkal for
Popular Prakashan Pvt. Ltd.
35-C, Pt. Madan Mohan Malaviya Marg
Popular Press Building,Tardeo,
Mumbai 400 034

Author's Note

It delights, it soothes, it satisfies, it teases. It is pure pleasure. It gives meal a sense of completion. A fine dessert is one of the richest gastronomical experiences possible. The word *dessert* is derived from the French *desservir,* which means to clear the table. Indeed the table is usually cleared to make way for the grand finale of the meal. It is the last course your guests will have before they depart, therefore it should be extraordinary to leave a lasting impression.

Various desserts are appealing to me at different times and for different reasons. This book contains 234 of my best recipes. Each one has been personally tried and tested. Some are quick and easy, some are elaborate but spectacular. There are eight sections to this book for easy reference. It records some traditional desserts like Sachertorte from Vienna, Black Forest Gâteau from Germany, Crème Brulee from France, Cheesecakes from America, Tiramisu from Italy, Phirni and Rosogolla from India, English Trifle, Baklava from the Middle East and some easy ones like Coffee Walnut Gâteau. Chocolate Crunch Pie, Chocolate Brownies, Shrikhand, and Apple Pie. The possibilities are endless. I have tried to cover the best desserts from all over the world, so go ahead and take the plunge; begin indulging your sweet tooth.

None of these are very difficult to make. The key is to read the recipe very carefully before beginning, to be sure that you have all the equipments and ingredients at hand. Your dessert can be as good as the ingredients that go into it. Buy the best and the freshest. Cheap substitutions and imitation products always betray their value in the final result. A dessert should be an event—a celebration. A truly wonderful dessert should dazzle the eye, excite the mind, delight the palate, satisfy the craving and transport you to heaven! May it be the quintessential pièce de résistance! May you all enjoy them both in the preparation and in the plaudits you receive when you serve them.

I dedicate this book to all my friends whose love for desserts inspired me to compile this book and I thank them for their interest, support and eagerness to taste my recipes... Some of the very special ones are...

Dipak Tanna
Shahnaz Mahimtura
Dr. Sanjay Desai
Jyoti Sheth
Ravi Ruia
Vandana Kejriwal

Acknowledgements

My sincere thanks...

To the one above...who made me capable and strong.

My heartfelt thanks...

To my family...My husband, Mahendra Khatau, who has inspired me and always been there by my side and my three children, Priya, Shreya and Manish for their constant enthusiasm, help and support.

To my pillars of strength, my mother-in-law, Leela Khatau and my mother Sudha Sampat.

To my sister-in law, Ameeta Thackersey and brother-in- law, Jagdish Thackersey for their special help and support all through out.

To my sister Raksha, for her help in computer work.

To my friends Vandana Kejriwal, Niti Desai, Supriya Desai and Tanvi Desai for their help during the photo shoot.

To Harsha Bhatkal, Swapna Shinde and all of those at Popular Prakashan.

To my dedicated staff at home, Gopinath, Mahadev, Vinod, Naresh and Dattu.

To all my close friends and my cooking class students who cheered me on.

And lastly to all of you who bought my book and who enjoy cooking for your family and friends.

Contents

Basic Recipes

Cakes and Gâteaux

Cold Desserts

Hot Desserts

Pastries and Pies

Fruits, Ice-creams and Sorbets

Custards, Mousses and Souffles

Cookies and Confectionaries

Glossary

Basic Recipes

A strong base results in stronger foundation. So let's get our basics right!

Basic Crêpe Recipe

Makes 12-15 6" diameter Crêpes

INGREDIENTS

1½ cups	*Plain flour, sieved*
2	*Eggs*
1 tbsp	*Sugar with a pinch of salt*
100 gms (½ cup)	*Whole wheat flour (sieved)*
300 ml (½ pint)	*Milk*
2 tbsps	*Butter, melted*
1 tbsp	*Grand Mariner of extra liqueur (optional)*
Oil	*For frying*

METHOD

Beat the eggs with salt or sugar and then stir in the sieved flour. Pour the milk in and beat it to a thin smooth cream. You could add a tablespoon of Grand Mariner if you wish. Set aside to rest for 20 minutes. Put a thick-based frying pan, about seven inches in diameter over moderate heat and brush it with oil. Pour two tablespoons of the batter into the pan and swirl it around so that the mixture spreads evenly over the base of the pan. Let it cook for three to four minutes and turn it over gently with a spatula and cook on the other side. The pan should not be too hot before you pour the butter. Continue until all the mixture is used up. Place the prepared crêpes on a large lightly buttered plate and cover them with butter paper, until ready to use.

Basic Sponge Cake

Makes ¼ kg sponge cake

INGREDIENTS

85 gms	*Plain flour, sift before measuring*
¾ tsp	*Baking powder*
3	*Eggs (large), at room temperature*
115 gms	*Powdered sugar*
2 tbsps	*Hot water*
4 tbsps	*Melted butter*

METHOD

Sieve flour and baking powder together and set aside. Grease and dust a seven inches round tin. Preheat the oven to 200° C or 400° F. In a medium-sized bowl, beat eggs and sugar until light and fluffy. Fold in gently the sieved flour with a metal spoon little at a time. Add hot water and butter ensuring that the lightness of the batter is secured. Pour this mixture in the prepared tin and bake in the preheated oven for 15 minutes or until golden in colour and the mixture leaves the sides of the pan. Remove from oven and cool for two-three minutes and invert on a wire rack and cool. Use as required.

For Chocolate sponge cake: Reduce the plain flour by two tablespoons and add two tablespoons of cocoa powder and sieve along with the flour.

Eggless Sponge Cake

Makes 1/4 kg sponge cake

INGREDIENTS

140 gms	*Plain flour, sift before measuring*
1½ tsps	*Baking powder*
½ tsp	*Soda bi-carbonate*
4 tbsps	*Melted butter*
5 tbsps	*Hot water*
200 gms	*Sweetened condensed milk*
1 tsp	*Vanilla essence*

METHOD

Sieve the flour, baking powder and soda together in a bowl. Grease and dust a six inches round cake tin. Mix the remaining ingredients in a bowl and beat with an electric beater. Fold in the flour mixture in the liquid, little at a time. Pour this mixture in a greased tin and bake in a hot oven at 200° C or 400° F for 10 minutes. Reduce the temperature to 150° C or 325° F for another 10 minutes. Remove from oven and cool for two-three minutes and invert on a wire rack and cool. Use as required.

Eggless Chocolate Cake

Serves 6-8

INGREDIENTS

1½ cups	*Plain flour, sieved*
3 tbsps	*Cocoa powder*
1 tsp	*Baking powder*
½ tsp	*Baking soda*
¼ tsp	*Salt*
1 cup (each)	*Powdered sugar and water*
6 tbsps	*Melted butter*
1 tsp	*Vanilla essence*
1 tsp	*Oil to grease and dust the tin*
1 tbsp	*Plain flour to grease and dust the tin*

METHOD

Preheat the oven to 350°F. Grease and dust an eight inch square or round tin. Sieve the flour, sugar, cocoa, baking powder, soda and salt together in a bowl. Add water, butter, and vanilla. Mix well. Pour the mixture and bake it in preheated oven for 25 minutes. Remove and set aside to cool slightly and then invert on a rack. Cool completely. Use as required.

Sweet Short Crust Pastry

Makes one 8"-9" pastry

INGREDIENTS

1 cup	*Sifted plain flour*	
½ cup	*Cold butter*	
2 tbsps	*Powdered sugar*	
4-5 tbsps	*Cold water*	*OR*
1 large	*Egg + 1 tbsp cold water*	
A pinch of salt		

METHOD

Sift flour, salt and sugar together in a bowl. Cut butter into pieces and rub it through the flour with the help of two forks. The mixture should resemble breadcrumbs. Make a well in the center and break an egg or add cold water and gradually mix the flour to form a ball. Do not overwork the dough. Refrigerate for thirty minutes before rolling.

Classic English Custard

Makes 2 cups

INGREDIENTS

4	*Egg yolks*
1 ¾ cups	*Milk*
6 tbsps	*Powdered sugar*
1 piece	*Vanilla bean OR*
1 tsp	*Vanilla essence*

METHOD

Beat the egg yolks and sugar until light. In a heavy saucepan, heat the milk on a slow flame. Add vanilla bean. Gently pour the egg yolk mixture and stir continuously. Cook until the mixture thickens. Ensure the mixture does not curdle. Remove from stove, discard vanilla bean (if using) or add vanilla essence now. Pass it through a sieve and serve warm or cold with steamed pudding or stewed fruits. If serving cold, cover the surface with buttered paper or plastic wrap.

Suzette Sauce

Makes 2½ cups

INGREDIENTS

2 cups	*Sweet-orange marmalade*
¼ cup	*Cointreau or Grand Marnier*
⅓ cup	*Brandy*
¼ cup	*Cold butter, cut into pieces*

METHOD

In a small saucepan, combine marmalade, liqueur and brandy. Cook over medium heat until marmalade melts. Remove from heat and add butter; stir quickly until butter melts. Serve warm or room temperature with ice cream.

Chocolate Fudge Velvet Sauce

Makes about 1¾ cups

INGREDIENTS

½ cup	Cocoa
1 cup	Sugar
¾ cup	Fresh cream
2 tbsps	Butter
A pinch of salt	

METHOD

In a medium heavy saucepan, combine cocoa, sugar and salt and heat on medium flame and stir until mixture is smooth. Gradually stir in the cream. Bring the mixture to a boil, stirring constantly. Reduce the heat to low. Cook for two minutes, stirring frequently. Remove from heat. Add butter and whisk until it melts. Serve warm. The sauce will thicken as it cools. Cover and refrigerate. You can store it for one month. To reheat, warm it in a double boiler.

It is delicious when served with orange, cherry or vanilla ice cream.

Tangy Lemon Butter Sauce

Serves 4

INGREDIENTS

3	Lemons
⅓ cup	Brown sugar
¼ cup	Butter
3 tbsps	Limoncello or Cointreau (optional)
Juice of 1 orange	

METHOD

Grate rind of one lemon and take out the juice of all three lemons. Place sugar, half of lemon juice and lemon rind in a saucepan. Heat gently, stirring till sugar has dissolved. Bring to a boil and cook until the syrup starts to turn golden on the edges. Add the remaining ingredients and cook, stirring frequently, until butter has melted. Stir in the liqueur (if using). Let the sauce bubble for two to three minutes. Serve warm with ice cream.

Coffee Walnut Sauce

Makes 1¼ cups

INGREDIENTS

60 gms	*Butter*
¼ cup	*Walnuts, chopped*
¼ cup	*Icing sugar*
3 tbsps	*Instant coffee*
1 tsp	*Hot water*
½ cup	*Thick cream*
3 tbsps	*Tia Maria or kahlua*

METHOD

In a small sauce pan, combine butter, sugar, coffee, hot water and cream. Stir constantly without boiling. Add walnuts and liqueur. Stir until smooth and mix well. Serve hot.

This sauce is suitable for chocolate or butterscotch ice cream or to pour over pancakes.

Hazelnut Sauce

Serves 4-6

INGREDIENTS

¼ cup	*Toasted and chopped hazelnuts*
⅔ cup	*Brown Sugar*
½ cup + 3 tbsps	*Water*
2 ½ tbsps	*Butter*

Grated rind of one small Orange

METHOD

Mix sugar and half a cup of water in a sauce pan and heat gently until sugar dissolves. Bring to a boil rapidly until syrup has turned golden. Remove from fire and cool over a bowl of cold water. Add butter, three tablespoon of water, hazelnuts and orange rind to the syrup and return to heat. Cook gently, stirring until smooth. Serve warm with fruits, icecreams or crèpes.

Glossy Chocolate Sauce

Makes 1½ cups

INGREDIENTS

½ cup	*Sugar*
¼ cup	*Water*
150 gms	*Semi-sweet chocolate, chopped*
2 tbsps	*Butter*
2 tbsps	*Brandy or orange juice*

METHOD

Heat the sugar gently with water in a heavy saucepan until it melts. Add the chocolate, few squares at a time, until it melts. Add butter to this mixture. Do not allow the sauce to boil. Stir in the brandy or orange juice and mix well. Serve warm with ice cream.

Tip : Over-cooking of chocolate results in lack of luster in the sauce.

Butterscotch Sauce

Serves 4-6

INGREDIENTS

6 tbsps	*Butter*
¾ cup (each)	*Dark brown sugar*
¾ cup	*Thick milk*
½ cup	*Hazelnuts or almonds, toasted and chopped*

METHOD

Melt butter and sugar in a heavy saucepan and bring to a boil. Boil for two minutes. Remove from stove and cool slightly. Heat the milk separately just below boiling point. Gradually stir it into the sugar mixture. Cook over low heat for two minutes, stirring frequently. Add the nuts and mix well. Serve hot with ice cream, pancake or waffles.

Cakes and Gâteaux

A baked flour confection sweetened with sugar, honey, etc., is known to be the food for Gods by Greeks and Egyptians in ancient times. For centuries, mankind has been using cakes in celebrations such as birthdays, weddings and anniversaries. So let's create magic with the freshest ingredients and perfect recipes and earn the reputation of a blue-ribbon baker.

Chocolate Sponge with Blackcurrant Mousse

Serves 6-8

INGREDIENTS

1 7" round	*Chocolate sponge cake (recipe on page 20)*
2-3 tbsps	*Powdered sugar mixed with 1/4 cup of water*
100 gms packet	*Blackcurrant jelly*
1 cup	*Whipping cream*
1 tbsp	*Lemon juice*

To Garnish

Whipped cream and a few dark grapes

METHOD

Cut the cake horizontally in two parts. Place the top part on a serving plate. Soak with sugar water. Set aside. Mix jelly with half a cup of water. Leave to set slightly. Whip the cream with lemon juice until it becomes double in volume. Whisk the jelly till light and frothy. Combine carefully with the cream. Spread half of this mixture on the halved cake. Soak the remaining cake with sugar water and place it over the mousse. Spread remaining mousse over the cake and smoothen the surface. Arrange grapes on top and garnish with cream. Chill until ready to serve.

Almond and Chocolate Gâteau

Serves 8-10

INGREDIENTS

1 piece	*4"x12" rectangle sponge cake*
For Chocolate cream	
100 gms	*Plain chocolate, broken into pieces*
3 tbsps	*Butter*
2/3 cup	*Fresh cream*
3 tbsps	*Powdered sugar*
For Orange cream	
125 gms	*Butter*
3/4 cup	*Fresh cream*
3 tbsps	*Powdered sugar*
Grated rind of 1/2 an orange	
To Garnish	
3 tbsps	*Thinly-sliced almonds*
3 tbsps	*Icing sugar*

METHOD

Cut the cake into half and set aside. Melt the chocolate in a double-boiler. Add butter and stir till melted. Cool. Whip the cream until thick, then fold it into the lukewarm chocolate until smooth and shiny. Beat the butter until light for the orange cream. Whip the cream with sugar until thick, then add to the butter a little at a time, mixing gently. Stir in the orange rind. Place second half of the sponge cake on a tray and spread with the chocolate cream. Top it with the other half slice and either pipe or spread orange cream. Garnish with icing sugar and sliced almonds. Refrigerate. Slice vertically and serve chilled.

Coffee Walnut Gâteau

Serves 6-8

INGREDIENTS

1 ¼ kg	*Plain sponge cake*
3 cups	*Whipping cream*
½ cup	*Powdered sugar*
200 gms	*Philadelphia cream cheese*
½ cup	*Strong coffee*
1 tbsp	*Coffee essence*
½ cup	*Chopped and toasted walnuts*
½ cup	*Brown sugar*

Butter to grease the tray

To Garnish

Whipped cream and halved walnuts.

METHOD

Melt sugar in a thick pan till golden colour. Remove from stove and add walnuts. Mix well. Turn this out on a greased tray and set aside to cool. Coarsely powder the caramalized walnuts. Slice the cake into three to four equal parts horizontally. Mix strong coffee with essence. Soak cake slices with half of the coffee mixture. Set aside. Beat the cream cheese with half a cup of sugar and remaining coffee mixture. Set aside. Whip the cream with sugar until soft peaks form. Remove three-fourth cup of cream for decoration on top. Gently fold in the powdered walnut into the beaten cream. Place one slice of cake on a serving plate and spread cream and walnut mixture. Place another slice on top and spread cream cheese mixture evenly. And finally place the third slice and top it with the cream mixture again. If you have the fourth layer then cover it on the top and then garnish with whipped cream and halved walnuts. Refrigerate until ready to serve.

Kiwi Black Forest Cake

Serves 8

INGREDIENTS

1	*7" round chocolate sponge cake (recipe on page 20)*
300 gms	*Fresh cream*
6 + 2 tbsps	*Powdered sugar*
2	*Kiwis, peeled and sliced*
1 tsp	*Lemon juice*

To Garnish

Grated chocolate and whipped cream

METHOD

Cut the sponge cake horizontally through the centre and soak it with sugar water made with two tablespoons of sugar dissolved in three tablespoons of water. Beat the cream over a bowl of ice cubes. Gradually add sugar and finally add lemon juice to it and continue beating till it becomes stiff. Spread half of the cream over the bottom half of the cake and arrange half of the sliced kiwi on the cream. Cover this with the other half of the cake. Pipe or spread the remaining cream and arrange the remaining kiwi on top. Decorate with chocolate and chill until ready to serve.

Coffee Walnut Gâteau

Kiwi Black Forest Cake

Mascarpone Cheesecake

Mascarpone Cheesecake

Serves 6-8

INGREDIENTS

For the Base

150 gms	*Oreo Cookies, toasted*
150 gms	*Almond macaroons or cookies, toasted*
3 tbsps	*Butter*
3 tbsps	*Powdered sugar*

For the Cheesecake

100 gms	*Mascarpone*
100 gms	*Philadelphia cream cheese*
200 gms	*Condensed milk*
100 gms	*Whipping cream*
½ cup	*Semi-sweet chocolate chips*
4 tsps	*Gelatine, mixed with six tablespoons of cold water*
1 tbsp	*Kahlua (optional)*

To Garnish

Grated chocolate, chocolate chips and whipped cream

METHOD

For the Base

Crush both the biscuits in a blender to crumble them, or you could break the biscuits up onto a greaseproof paper, cover them with another piece and firmly push a rolling pin to and fro until the biscuits become crumbs. Melt butter in a saucepan and add biscuit crumbs and sugar in it. Mix well. Remove from stove and line the base and sides of a loose bottom cake tin approx imately 9-10 inches with the biscuit crumbs and press it with the back of your hand to spread evenly. Bake it in hot oven at 350°F for 5-7 minutes. Set aside.

For the Cheesecake

Cook gelatine mixture on a slow flame, until transparent. Remove from stove and cool completely. Pass it thorough a fine sieve. Set aside. Place the Philadelphia cream cheese and condensed milk in the liquidizer jar. Blend until mixed. Turn it out in a large bowl. Set aside. In another small bowl, beat whipping cream until thick. Gently fold in the Mascarpone cheese. Add this to the Philadelphia cream cheese mixture. Gently fold in chocolate chips and Kahlua. Fold in gelatine mixture in a thin stream. Pour the mixture onto the prepared cookie crust and freeze for two hours or until set. Remove from the tin onto a serving plate and garnish with grated chocolate, chocolate chips, and whipped cream. Serve chilled.

Chocolate Mousse Cake

Serves 6-8

INGREDIENTS

1 7" round *Chocolate sponge cake (recipe on page 20)*

For the Mousse

1 tbsp	*Cold water*
1 tbsp	*Powdered gelatine*
¼ cup	*Hot water*
½ cup	*Cocoa powder*
1 cup	*Powdered sugar*
2 cups	*Whipping cream*
1 tsp	*Vanilla essence*

To garnish

Sliced almonds and chocolate curls

METHOD

Sprinkle gelatine over cold water and set aside for 5-7 minutes. In a saucepan mix cocoa, sugar and hot water. Cook gently until smooth. Add gelatine mixture and mix well. Pass the mixture through a sieve and cool over a bowl of ice. Add the vanilla. Whip the cream until soft peaks form. Fold it into the cocoa mixture and chill. Cut the sponge cake into half from the middle. Place bottom half onto a seven inches tin; cut side up. Soak the cake with half of the syrup. Pour chocolate mousse over it and spread evenly. Soak the other half of the cake with remaining syrup and cover on top of the mousse with soaked side down. Cover the tin and freeze until the mousse is set. Invert the cake onto a serving plate and garnish with almonds, whipped cream and chocolate curls. Chill until ready to serve.

Black Forest Cherry Gâteau

Serves 10

INGREDIENTS

For the Chocolate Sponge Cake

6 large — *Eggs*
240 gms — *Powdered sugar*
1 tsp — *Vanilla essence*
6 tbsps — *Plain flour*
4 tbsps — *Cocoa*

For the Filling

200 gms — *Fresh Morello cherries l*
180 gms — *Sugar l OR*
2½ cups — *Water l*
1 tin (240 gms) — *Tinned cherries*

For the Syrup

1 cup — *Juice from the cherries or the liquid from the tin*
2 tbsps — *Powdered sugar*
½ cup — *Kirsch (cherry liqueur)*

For the Topping

3 cups — *Whipping cream*
8 tbsps — *Icing sugar*
1 tsp — *Cherry brandy (optional)*

To Garnish

1 cup — *Chocolate shavings*

METHOD

For the Cake

Grease and dust two deep-sided nine inches cake tins. Preheat the oven to 180°C or 350°F. In a large bowl beat the eggs and sugar with vanilla until thick and fluffy. Sift together flour and cocoa. Fold into the egg mixture, little at a time, scrapping the bowl from the sides with a rubber spatula. Divide the mixture between two tins and bake in the centre of the oven for 20-25 minutes. Remove and cool for five minutes and then turn it out on cooling rack.

For the filling

Remove stalks and stones from fresh cherries and put them in a saucepan with water and sugar. Bring to a boil and simmer for five minutes, uncovered. Strain and dry the cherries. Reserve the syrup.

For the Syrup

Measure syrup from the cherries to one cup; adjust with water if you run short. Put the syrup and two tablespoons of sugar in a saucepan and heat gently till sugar dissolves. Remove from stove and add Kirsch. Soak both the cakes with this syrup. Set aside.

For the Topping

Beat the chilled cream over a bowl of ice with sugar until thick. Add cherry brandy while beating (if using).

To Assemble the Gâteau

Place one soaked cake on a serving platter. Spread it with a layer of cream, one-fourth thick. Sprinkle the surface with cherries, leaving a border of cream around the edges. Gently slide the other cake onto the first one. Cover the cake with half a inch layer of cream. Coat the sides of the gateau with remaining cream. With fingertips, trim the sides of the cake with chocolate shavings, pressing them into the cream. Decorate the top with the cream using a piping bag and fluted nozzle. Fill the centre with the remaining cherries and place them in between the florets of the cream. Refrigerate until served.

Chocolate Bar-Filled Chocolate Cupcakes

Makes 24 cupcakes

INGREDIENTS

For Chocolate Bar Filling

200 gms	*Cream cheese*
1/3 cup	*Powdered sugar*
1/4 cup	*Cream*
1 bar (175 gms)	*Milk chocolate, cut into 1/4" pieces*

For Chocolate cupcakes

3 cups	*Plain flour, sieved*
2 cups	*Powdered sugar*
2/3 cup	*Cocoa*
2/3 cup	*Salad oil*
2 tsps	*Baking soda*
2 tsps	*Vanilla essence*
1 tsp	*Salt*
2 cups	*Cold water*
2 tbsps	*White vinegar*
2 bars	*Milk chocolate, cut into 2"x2" squares*

METHOD

For the chocolate bar-filling

Beat cream cheese, sugar, cream and salt in a small bowl until smooth and creamy. Stir in chocolate bar pieces. Set aside.

For the cupcakes

Heat the oven to 350°F. Line muffin cups with 2"-2½" diameter paper baking cups. In a large bowl mix together flour, sugar, cocoa, baking soda and salt. Add water, oil, vinegar and vanilla. Beat on medium speed for two minutes. Fill muffin cups two-thirds full with batter. Spoon one tablespoon of bar chocolate filling into the centre of each cupcake. Bake for 20-25 minutes or until wooden pick comes out clean. Cool completely on a wire rack. Top each cake with a chocolate bar piece.

Coffee Roulade

Serves 8-10

INGREDIENTS

For the Roulade

4	*Eggs, separated*
½ cup	*Castor sugar*
½ cup	*Plain flour, well sieved*
3 tbsps	*Warm water*
½ tsp	*Baking powder*
A pinch of salt	
1 tbsp	*Camp coffee essence*

You will need a 12" x 8" x ½" deep tray lined with greaseproof paper and coated with melted butter.

For the Filling

400 gms	*Fresh cream*
3-4 tbsps	*Sugar*
1 tbsp	*Essence*
2 tbsps	*Instant coffee mixed with 1 tbsp of hot water*
1 tbsp	*Kahlua or Tia Maria liqueur (optional)*

To Garnish

Flakes of almond or chocolate pieces

METHOD

For the Roulade

Preheat the oven to 180°C. Place the egg yolks in a slightly warm bowl and beat with an electric mixer for five minutes. Add the sugar gradually, beating well after each addition. Reduce the speed of the mixer to number one and add the flour mixture, alternating it with water. Beat gently until all the mixture is absorbed. Beat the egg whites until stiff and fold in to the mixture with a metal spoon in a circular motion, till absorbed. Quickly pour the mixture into the prepared tray and bake in the oven for about 15-18 minutes. Do not over bake. Now turn it out onto a sugared foil or a dampened tea towel and roll it gently. Set aside to cool.

For the Filling

Beat the cream till thick, add sugar, coffee essence, instant coffee and Kahlua. Continue beating till thick. Open up the roulade and spread the flavored cream onto it and re roll carefully. Transfer to a serving tray and decorate as desired. Chill until ready to serve.

Chocolate Swiss Roll

Serves 8

INGREDIENTS

3/4 cup	*Plain flour*
1/2 tsp	*Baking powder*
2 tbsps	*Cocoa powder*
A pinch of salt	
3 large	*Eggs, separated*
1/2 cup	*Castor sugar*
1/2 tsp	*Vanilla essence*
For the filling	
1 1/2 cups	*Whipping cream*
3/4 cup	*Chopped cooking chocolate*
2-3 tbsps	*Icing sugar*
1 tbsp	*Brandy (optional)*
To garnish	
Chopped chocolate and whipped cream	

METHOD

Line, grease and dust a 8x12 inch Swiss roll tin. Sieve plain flour with baking powder, cocoa and salt. Whisk the eggs and sugar together in a large bowl until light and fluffy. Gently fold in the flour mixture. Turn the mixture into the lined tin and smooth the surface. Bake in a preheated oven for 10-12 minutes or until springy to touch. Turn out onto lightly sugared, greaseproof paper or foil placed on a slightly damp, clean cloth and remove the lining paper. Roll up tightly from the short edge with the sugared paper inside. Leave to cool for about 20 minutes. Unroll the sponge and remove the paper.

For the Filling

Melt the chocolate over boiling water. Remove and cool to room temperature. Set aside. Whip the cream with icing sugar in a stainless steel bowl over a bowl of ice until soft peaks form. Gently fold in the cooled chocolate and brandy (if using).

Spread evenly the chocolate cream over the sponge. Carefully roll the sponge with the filling, as tightly as possible. Place it on a serving tray. Garnish with chopped chocolate and swirls of cream. Chill until ready to serve.

Candy Bar Cake

Serves 8

INGREDIENTS

For the Cake

1½ cups	*Plain flour, sift before measuring*
1 cup	*Powdered sugar*
1 tsp	*Baking soda*
A pinch of salt	
⅓ cup (each)	*Cocoa and oil*
1 cup	*Cold water*
1 tsp	*Vanilla essence*

For the Frosting

½ cup (each)	*Cream cheese and whipping cream*
¼ cup	*Powdered sugar*
100 gms	*Chopped candy bar of your choice (such as Mars)*

To Garnish

Chopped 1 chocolate bar and whipped cream

METHOD

For the Cake

Sieve all the dry ingredients together. Mix oil, vanilla, and cold water. Place dry ingredients in one bowl and add the liquid ingredients with electric beater on lowest speed until all the ingredients are well blended. Pour this in a 8-9" round tin and bake in hot oven at 350° F for 30-35 minutes. The top of the cake should spring back on touching. Remove from the tin and set aside to cool for 10 minutes. Invert on a wire rack and allow the cake to cool completely. Slice the cake from the centre and soak with sugar water.

For the Frosting

In a medium bowl, beat cream cheese and powdered sugar until light. In another bowl whip the cream until soft peaks are formed. Fold in the cream and candy bar pieces into the cream cheese mixture. Set aside.

To Assemble

Place the top half of the cake onto a serving plate. Spread half the frosting evenly. Cover with remaining frosting on top. Garnish with chopped chocolate and whipped cream. Refrigerate until ready to serve.

Candy Bar Cake

Chocolate Swiss Roll

Orange Cake

Piña Colada Cake

Orange Cake

Serves 6

INGREDIENTS

1 cup	*Plain flour*
½ tsp (each)	*Baking powder and soda*
A pinch of salt	
½ cup	*Powdered sugar*
¼ cup (each)	*Butter and thick cream*
1 tsp (each)	*Grated Orange rind and orange essence*
⅓ cup	*Orange juice*
For the frosting	
1 tbsp	*Butter*
¾ cup	*Icing sugar*
Orange juice	
To Garnish	
Orange slices or halved walnuts	

METHOD

Sieve together plain flour, baking powder, soda, salt and sugar. In another bowl, beat butter on medium speed. Add orange rind and juice. Fold in dry ingredients alternating with cream. Pour the mixture in greased 7" round tin. Bake in a hot oven at 150°C for 25-30 minutes or until the top is golden. Remove and cool on a rack.

For the Frosting

Beat butter until soft. Gradually beat in icing sugar and just enough orange juice to make the mixture into soft spreading consistency. Garnish with orange slices and walnuts. Cut into wedges and serve.

Piña Colada Cake

Serves 6-8

INGREDIENTS

1 -7" round	*Plain sponge cake*
¼ cup	*Sugar, dissolved in ½ cup of water OR*
1 tbsp	*Lemon juice*
¼ cup	*White rum, or water*
2 tbsps	*Sugar*

For Pina colada frosting

1 cup	*Chopped pineapple*
1 cup	*Coconut cream*
2 tbsps	*Corn flour and*
2 tbsps	*Powdered sugar*
1 cup	*Whipping cream*
1 tsp	*Lemon or pineapple essence*

To Garnish

2-3 slices of pineapple, thinly sliced coconut and mint leaves

METHOD

Slice the cake horizontally into two parts. Place the top half down, cut side up, on a serving plate. Mix sugar, water or rum and lemon juice. Soak the cake in this syrup.

For Frosting

In a small saucepan, mix coconut cream, sugar and corn flour. Heat gently until thick. Remove and cool completely. Whip the cream to soft peaks and add lemon essence. Fold in the pineapple pieces and thickened coconut cream.

To frost the cake, pour half of the frosting to the soaked cake. Sandwich it with the other half. Top it with the remaining frosting. Garnish with pineapple slices, coconut and mint leaves. Chill until ready to serve.

The Cheesecake

Serves 8-10

INGREDIENTS

For the Base

300 gms	*Digestive biscuits, slightly toasted*
50 gms	*Melted butter*
$1/4$ cup	*Powdered sugar*

For the Cheesecake

250 gms	*Philadelphia cream cheese*
3	*Eggs, separated*
100 gms	*Castor sugar*
300 ml	*Double cream*
$4\frac{1}{2}$ tsps	*Gelatine mixed with 5 tbsps liquid*

To Garnish

Whipped cream and relevant fruit slices

METHOD

Crumble the biscuits with a rolling pin or in the food processor. Put crumbs into a bowl and fold in the melted butter. Line the base and sides of a loose-bottomed cake tin approximately 9-10 inches with the biscuit crumbs and press with the back of your hand to spread evenly. Bake this in an oven at 350°F for 15 minutes and leave it to cool.

Mix the gelatine with water or any other liquid, according to the flavour of the cheesecake you wish to use and soak for five minutes. Gently heat on a slow flame. Cook until the liquid is transparent, remove from the stove and cool the mixture, stirring constantly. Set aside. Lightly beat the egg yolks and beat these into the cream cheese with the sugar and then lightly-whipped double cream.

Add the relevant flavourings (see individual recipes). Fold in the stiffly beaten egg whites. Now reheat the gelatine over very low heat and melt the mixture. Use a very fine sieve through which you pass the gelatine. Fold straight into the cheese mixture by making gentle sweeping movements resembling the number eight. Pour the mixture onto the cooled biscuit base and place it in the fridge to set. When it is firm, loosen the sides of the cake from the tin and simply push the base upwards and discard the ring of the tin. Place this on a decorative plate and pipe some fresh cream and pieces of the relevant fruit or flavoring used for the cheesecake. Chilled until ready to serve.

Flavouring Suggestion

LEMON CHEESECAKE: Fold in the juice and rind of two lemons into the basic mixture. You may also add lemon liquor with the juice.

KIWI CHEESECAKE: You will need five Kiwi fruits. Liquidize two fruits with one tablespoon of Kiwi liqueur and 1 tbsp icing sugar. Line cooled base with extra slices of kiwi and fill half the cheese mixture. As it sets, spread further kiwi slices on the top and then cover with remaining mixture. Decorate with sweetened cream and kiwi slices or an orchid flower in the centre.

STRAWBERRY CHEESECAKE: You will need 500 gms of strawberries. Liquidize half of the strawberries with one tablespoon of brandy and one tablespoon of icing sugar. Proceed the same way as the kiwi recipe.

COFFEE, RUM AND WALNUT CHEESECAKE: Add two tablespoons of Camp coffee essence and two tablespoons of any coffee liqueur to the basic recipe. Mix the gelatine with three tablespoons of rum and two tablespoons of water. Line the cooled crumb base with two tablespoons of chopped walnuts and pour half the cheesecake mixture. When set, add more walnuts and the balance mixture. Decorate with piped cream and toasted walnuts. Serve chilled.

Eggless Cheesecake

Serves 6-8

INGREDIENTS

For the Base

200 gms	*Digestive biscuits*
50 gms	*Melted butter*
¼ cup	*Powdered sugar*

For the Cheesecake

200 gms	*Philadelphia cream cheese*
200 gms	*Condensed milk*
100 gms	*Fresh cream*
1 tbsp	*Lemon juice*
5 gms	*China grass mixed with 5 tbsps of water OR*
4 tsps	*Gelatine mixed with ¼ cup of liquid*

To Garnish

Whipped cream and relevant topping

METHOD

For the Base

Crumble the biscuits with a rolling pin or in food processor. Melt butter in a saucepan and add biscuit crumbs and sugar. Mix well. Remove from stove and line the base and sides of a loose bottom cake tin approximately 9-10" with the biscuit crumbs and press it with the back of your hand to spread evenly. Bake it in hot oven at 350°F for 5-7 minutes and set aside to cool.

For the Cheesecake

Mix china grass or gelatine with water or preferred liquid and heat gently, stirring all the time. Remove from stove and set aside to cool. Strain the gelatine mixture through a fine sieve. Liquidize cream cheese and condensed milk in a blender and put in a large bowl. Beat the cream until thick and add to the cheese mixture and gently fold in the preferred flavoring spoon by spoon, in an upward movement, along with lemon juice. Add cooled gelatine mixture in a thin stream making sure each addition is incorporated. Mix well. Pour this mixture over the prepared and lined tin. Cover and chill in the refrigerator for 2-4 hours. Remove from the tin onto a serving plate and garnish with whipped cream and flavouring ingredient of your choice.

Note : For flavouring suggestions refer to the Cheesecake recipe.

Chocolate Cheesecake

Serves 6-8

INGREDIENTS

For the base

200 gms	Oreo cookies
50 gms	Melted butter
1/4 cup	Powdered sugar

For the cheesecake

200 gms	Philadelphia cream cheese
200 gms	Condensed milk
100 gms	Fresh cream
150 gms	Dark cooking chocolate, melted and cooled
5 gms	China grass mixed with 5 tbsps of water OR
3 tsps	Gelatine mixed with 1/4 cup of cold water
1 tsp	Vanilla essence

To Garnish

Whipped cream and chopped chocolate

METHOD

For the Base

Crumble the biscuits with a rolling pin or in food processor. Turn the crumbs out into a bowl and fold in the melted butter and sugar. Layer the base and sides of a nine inch loose bottom tin with the crumb mixture and press it with the back of your hand to spread evenly. Bake it in hot oven at 350°F for five to seven minutes and set aside to cool.

For the Cheesecake

Mix china grass or gelatine with water and gently heat until transparent. Set aside to cool. Strain the gelatine mixture through a fine sieve. Liquidize cream cheese and condensed milk in a blender jar and put in a large bowl. Beat the cream until thick. Fold in the melted chocolate and vanilla. Add this to the cheese mixture. Pour into the prepared and lined tin. Cover and chill in the refrigerator for two-four hours. Remove from the tin onto a serving plate and garnish with whipped cream and chopped chocolate.

Chocolate-Blackcurrant Swirl Cheesecake

Serves 8-10

INGREDIENTS

For Chocolate Crumb Crust

1½ cups	*Vanilla Wafer crumbs*
¼ cup	*Melted butter*
6 tbsps	*Powdered sugar and cocoa*

For the Cheesecake

200 gms	*Cream cheese and condensed milk*
½ cup	*Whipping cream*
1 cup	*Black currant pulp*
4 tsps	*Gelatine powder mixed with 5 tablespoons of water*

For the Topping

¼ cup (each)	*Black currant jam and water*
1 tbsp (each)	*Corn flour and lemon juice*

To Garnish: *Whipped cream*

METHOD

For the Crumb Crust

In a saucepan mix butter and wafer crumbs. Add sugar and cocoa and mix well. Remove from stove and press this onto 9" loose bottom pan. Bake in a preheated oven for 10 minutes and cool.

For the Cheese Cake

Melt the gelatine over medium heat until transparent. Cool. Mix cream cheese and condensed milk in a blender jar. Pour it out in a bowl and add the gelatine mixture in a thin stream. Fold in the whipped cream. Mix two-three tablespoons of this mixture to blackcurrant pulp. Spread half of the cheese mixture over cooled crumb crust and place dollops of blackcurrant pulp over it. Repeat this by pouring remaining cheese mixture and the pulp on top. Now swirl with a sharp knife to create a marble effect. Chill for four to five hours.

For the Topping

Mix all the ingredients together in a saucepan and gently cook until transparent. Remove from stove and cool. Transfer the cheesecake onto a serving plate. Cover the top with the cooled topping and garnish with whipped cream.

Mocha Cream
(Layered Coffee Cake)

Serves 6-8

INGREDIENTS

1	*8-9" plain sponge cake (recipe on page 20)*
1 cup	*Butter*
2 ½ cups	*Powdered sugar*
2 tbsps	*Camp coffee essence*
3 tbsps	*Instant coffee powder*
1 cup	*Hot water*

To Garnish

Slivered and toasted almonds.

METHOD

Make the cake a day before you make the pudding and refrigerate it. Cut the cake horizontally into four to five very thin slices. Make a coffee decoction by mixing hot water with the instant coffee and essence. Let the mixture cool. Beat the butter until light and fluffy. Add the sugar spoon by spoon, alternating with one small spoon of the coffee decoction until all the sugar is incorporated and the mixture is light and fluffy. Place the bottom layer of the cake on the serving dish and soak it in the coffee decoction. Spread a thin layer of the coffee cream. Even it out with a spatula. Place another slice of cake over it exactly in line with the first and repeat the earlier procedure until all the slices are used. After the last layer, frost the whole cake with the remaining coffee cream. Even it out and garnish with toasted almonds. Serve at room temperature.

Bailey's Irish Cream Torte

Serves 8

INGREDIENTS

1/4 kg	*Plain sponge cake*
2 tbsps	*Instant coffee mixed with 1/4 cup of hot water*
1 tbsp	*Camp coffee essence*
1/2 cup	*Toasted and ground almonds*
1 cup	*Butter*
2 1/4 cups	*Icing sugar*
1/4 cup	*Bailey's Irish cream liqueur OR*
1/3 cup	*Espresso coffee mixed with 1/2 teaspoon of vanilla essence*

To Garnish

Whipped cream, Coffee beans

METHOD

In a medium bowl, beat butter and slowly add icing sugar until all the sugar is incorporated. Add the liqueur, a spoon at a time, in between the sugar. Set aside. Slice the cake into three horizontal pieces. Mix strong coffee with Camp coffee essence. Soak one layer of sponge cake with one-third of this mixture. Place it on a serving plate. Spread one-third of the Bailey's frosting evenly on the cake. Sprinkle with half ground almonds. Soak second slice of cake with coffee decoction and place over the first one. Spread one-third of Bailey's frosting evenly on the sponge. Sprinkle the remaining ground almonds. Soak the third slice with coffee and place it on top, smooth side up. Spread remaining frosting evenly on top. Pipe decoratively with whipped cream and garnish with coffee beans or chopped chocolate. Chill until ready to serve.

Gingerbread

Serves 6-8

INGREDIENTS

1½ cups	Plain flour, sieved before measuring
¾ tsp (each)	Baking powder
¾ tsp	Baking soda
1 tsp	Salt
1 tbsp	Grated ginger
¾ tsp	Powdered cinnamon
⅓ cup	Salad oil
1 egg	Beaten OR
¼ cup	Condensed milk
⅓ cup	Brown sugar and
⅓ cup	Jaggery
½ cup	Boiling water

To Serve

Cinnamon flavoured whipped cream and icing sugar

METHOD

Sift together the first six ingredients. Place the mixture in a bowl. Make a well in the centre and pour oil, the brown sugar and then the condensed milk. Mix jaggery in boiling water and add to the batter. Beat until smooth. Pour into a greased 8" square or loaf tin. Bake in a preheated oven at 350°F or 180°c for 35-40 minutes. Cool in the tin for 10 minutes and turn it out on a wire wrack. Sprinkle liberally with icing sugar. Serve warm with cinnamon flavoured whipped cream.

Fruit and Praline Gâteau

Serves 6

INGREDIENTS

1- 7"round	*Sponge cake (recipe on page 20)*
2 cups	*Sliced fresh fruit of your choice (strawberries, kiwi, peaches, etc.)*
2 tbsps	*Powdered sugar (for the fruit)*
200 gms	*Whipping cream*
4 tbsps	*Powdered sugar (for the cream)*
2 tbsps	*Orange marmalade*
1 cup	*Praline powder*

METHOD

Cut the cake horizontally into two parts. Place the top half on a serving plate. Sprinkle sugar on the fruit and set aside for half an hour. Beat the cream with sugar in a chilled stainless steel bowl and refrigerate. Mix marmalade and syrup from the fruit. Spread this on the cake evenly. Mix half the fruit, half the cream and one-third of the praline powder. Spread this on the cake. Cover this with the other half of the sponge cake. Either pipe or spread the remaining cream on the top and the sides. Arrange the slices of fruits on the top and stick half of remaining praline on the sides of cake with a palate knife. Sprinkle remaining praline over the cake. Chill until ready to serve.

Praline powder

Gently heat three-fourth cup of whole sugar in a heavy saucepan. Add half a cup of cashew nuts or almonds. Cook until the mixture is rich brown in colour. Remove from the stove and spread the mixture on a baking tray. Set aside to cool. Coarsely powder when completely cold. Store in an air-tight jar.

Makes 1 cup

Carrot Cake

Serves 8

INGREDIENTS

2 cups	*Plain flour*
1 tsp (each)	*Baking powder, vinegar and powdered cinnamon*
½ tsp	*Soda*
A pinch of salt	
⅔ cup	*Butter*
1½ cups	*Sweetened condensed milk*
1 cup	*Finely grated carrots*
½ cup	*Ground almonds*
½ cup	*Thick buttermilk*

To Sprinkle

Icing sugar

METHOD

Sift together plain flour, baking powder, salt, soda and cinnamon powder. Toss grated carrot and ground almonds into the flour mixture. Beat butter and condensed milk in a mixing bowl until light. Fold in flour mixture and buttermilk alternately. Add vinegar along with a little water if the mixture feels dry. Pour into 9" round tin and bake in a hot oven at 400° F for 10 minutes and then at 300° F for 20 minutes or until the top is golden. Remove and cool in the pan for five minutes and then invert on the rack. Place the cake on a serving plate and sprinkle icing sugar. Serve warm.

Orange-Walnut Sponge Cake

Serves 6-8

INGREDIENTS

For the Cake

1 (250 gms)	*Plain sponge cake (recipe on page 20)*
1/3 cup	*Orange juice*
2 tbsps	*Powdered sugar*
1/4 cup	*Orange marmalade*

For Orange-Walnut Cream

1/2 cup	*Powdered sugar*
1/2 cup	*Orange juice*
3 tbsps	*Corn flour*
2 tsps	*Grated orange rind*
1 tbsp	*Lemon juice*
1 tsp	*Orange essence or orange liqueur*
1 1/2 cups	*Whipping cream*
1 cup	*Toasted and chopped walnuts*

To garnish

Whipped cream, orange slices and halved walnuts

METHOD

For the Cake

Mix orange juice, marmalade and sugar in a small saucepan and bring to a boil. Remove and cool the mixture. Slice the cake horizontally into three pieces. Place the top slice onto a serving plate. Soak the cake with one-third of the orange juice mixture. Spread one-third of the orange-walnut cream. Repeat the layers for the remaining two slices, ending with the orange cream. Arrange orange slices and walnut halves in a circular pattern. Keep in a cool place.

For Orange-Walnut Cream

Combine sugar, cornflour, orange rind, lemon juice and orange juice in a saucepan. Stir over low heat until thick. Stir over cold water to cool the mixture. Whip the cream until thick and fold it into the orange mixture along with walnuts and orange essence or liqueur.

Banana and Date Cake

Serves 6

INGREDIENTS

½ cup	*Butter, softened*
¾ cups	*Powdered sugar*
2 large	*Eggs*
1 large	*Banana, mashed*
¾ cup	*Plain flour*
½ tsp	*Baking powder*
½ tsp	*Soda*
¼ cup	*Ground almonds*
2 tbsps	*Milk*
½ cup	*Sliced black dates*

To Garnish

Icing sugar

To Serve

Whipped cream or custard

METHOD

Line 21 cms x10 cms size loaf pan with greaseproof paper. Cream butter and sugar in a bowl until light. Add eggs, one at a time. Stir in the mashed banana. Sieve the flour with baking powder and soda. Fold in the flour mixture, almonds and milk. Spoon half the batter in the prepared tin and spread evenly. Spread half the dates evenly. Top it with remaining batter and dates. Bake in a hot oven at 175°c for 30-35 minutes or until the top is golden. Cool slightly and remove from the pan. Sprinkle icing sugar on top and serve warm with whipped cream or custard.

Mango Upside-Down Cake

Serves 6-8

INGREDIENTS

2 cups	*Sliced ripe mango*
2 tbsps	*Lemon juice*
1 tbsp	*Butter*
⅓ cup	*Brown sugar*
For the Cake batter	
¼ cup	*Butter*
¾ cup	*Sugar*
1 large	*Egg*
½ cup	*Milk*
1¼ cup	*Plain flour sieved together*
2 tsps	*Baking powder sieved together*
¼ tsp	*Salt*

METHOD

Pour lemon juice over mango slices and let them stand for 15 minutes. Melt butter in a cake pan and add brown sugar. Cover with mango slices. Cream butter and sugar in a bowl until creamy. Add beaten egg. Add flour mixture and milk alternately with milk. Pour this mixture over mangoes and bake for 45 minutes at 375°F. Remove and turn it upside down on a plate. Serve warm.

Eggless version: Reduce sugar to half a cup, replace egg with one-fourth cup of condensed milk and add half a teaspoon of soda to the flour before sieving.

Sachertorte
(Vienna's Famous Chocolate Cake)

Serves 6-8

INGREDIENTS

165 gms	*Unsalted butter, softened*
165 gms	*Powdered sugar, sifted*
7	*Eggs, separated, whites stiffly beaten*
165 gms	*Dark cooking chocolate, melted*
100 gms	*Plain flour, sifted*
40 gms	*Ground almonds*
100 gms	*Apricot jam*
For the Icing	
100 ml	*Double cream*
2 tbsps	*Brandy*
100 gms	*Dark cooking chocolate, chopped*
To Garnish	

Chocolate leaves and icing sugar

METHOD

Grease and dust 7" round cake tin. In a medium bowl, beat butter until light and pale in colour. Add sugar and beat until fluffy. Add the egg yolks, one at a time, beating well after each addition. Stir in the melted chocolate. Sift the flour and almonds into the bowl and fold into the butter mixture. Gently fold in a third of stiffly beaten egg whites and then fold in the rest. Pour the mixture into the prepared tin and bake in preheated oven at 180° C or 350° F. for 40-45 minutes or until a skewer inserted comes out clean. Remove from the oven and set aside to cool for 10 minutes. Turn it out on a rack and cool completely. Warm the apricot jam and spread it over the top and sides of the cake. Set aside to set.

For the Icing

Place the cream and brandy in a saucepan and bring just to the boil. Add the chocolate pieces and stir until the chocolate melts and is smooth. Pour this over the cake evenly and leave to set, about 15 minutes. Garnish with chocolate leaves, dusted with icing sugar.

Cold Desserts

Coldness mutes tastes, so chilled desserts should be strongly flavoured. When it comes to keeping your "cool" in the kitchen during a big party, think of serving easy, delicious, frozen and refrigerated desserts to get a warm response from your guests.

Black Forest Trifle

Serves 4-6

INGREDIENTS

1/4 kg	*Chocolate sponge cake or Swiss roll*
5 tbsps	*Black cherry jam*
3 tbsps	*Cherry liqueur or cherry syrup*
500 gms	*Cherries, pitted, halved and sprinkled with 2 tbsps of sugar*
2 tbsps	*Corn flour*
2 tbsps	*Powdered sugar*
450 ml	*Milk*
1/3 cup	*Cream (for the custard)*
2/3 cup	*Fresh cream, whipped*

To Garnish

A few whole cherries and chocolate flakes

METHOD

Mix corn flour, sugar and milk in a saucepan over medium heat stirring constantly, until the mixture is thick. Remove from stove and cool. Add one-third cup of cream and mix well. Refrigerate until ready to use. Spread cherry jam on the sponge cake or fill inside the swiss roll. Cut the cake or the Swiss roll into half inch thick slices and arrange them at the bottom of a glass bowl. Sprinkle with cherry liqueur or cherry syrup. Layer the cherries over the cake. Pour cooled custard over the cherries and smoothen the surface. Spread three-fourth of the whipped cream over the custard and pipe the remaining on the edge of the bowl. Garnish with whole cherries and chocolate flakes. Chill for one-two hours before serving.

Note: You can divide the mixture and the cake in two and layer it twice.

Cappuccino Oreo Trifle

Serves 8

INGREDIENTS

½ cup	*Powdered sugar*
¼ cup	*Corn flour*
1 tbsp	*Instant coffee granules*
¼ cup	*Cream*
2½ cups	*Milk*
1 tbsp	*Camp coffee essence or vanilla essence*
1 tbsp	*Kahlua (optional)*
12-14 pieces	*Oreo cookies, divided*
1 cup	*whipping cream*

METHOD

Combine the first four ingredients in a bowl and stir well with a whisk. Boil milk on medium heat, until bubbles form. Remove from stove. Gradually add coffee mixture to boiling milk, stirring constantly. Return pan to stove and boil until mixture thickens. Simmer for two minutes and remove from stove and add coffee or vanilla essence and Kahlua (if using). Pour into a stainless steel bowl and place it on a bowl of ice water, stirring occasionally until mixture is cool. Coarsely chop half the cookies; fold chopped cookies and whipped cream into coffee mixture. Pour out the mixture into a serving bowl or spoon about half a cup mixture in individual parfait glasses. Chill for atleast two hours. Serve with remaining whole cookies on top.

Chocolate Chip Trifle

Serves 10-12

INGREDIENTS

For the Trifle

200 gms	Chocolate chip cookies
2 cups	Vanilla custard
2 cups	Sliced strawberries

For the Custard

1½ cups	Milk
6 tbsps	Powdered sugar
2 tbsps	Corn flour
1 tsp	Vanilla essence
½ cup	Fresh cream, beaten

To garnish

Fresh mint leaves, sweetened cream and halved strawberries

METHOD

For the custard

Boil milk with sugar. Dissolve corn flour with a little cold milk and add to the hot milk. Stir constantly till thick. Remove from the stove and set aside to cool. Add vanilla essence and beaten cream. Cool in the refrigerator.

For the Trifle

Crumble half the cookies. Sprinkle three-fourths of the crumbs on bottom of a deep 10 inch serving bowl. Top it with one-third of the custard. Place strawberries over the custard. Stand remaining cookies, face side out, along the inside of the dish. Spread remaining custard over the strawberries. Top it with the remaining crumbled cookies. Cover and refrigerate for 3-4 hours or overnight. Garnish with whipped cream, mint leaves and strawberries. Serve chilled.

Mocha Tiramisu Trifle

Serves 8

INGREDIENTS

2 (250 gms)	*Chocolate sponge cakes (recipe on page 20)*
1 tbsp	*Coffee liqueur (optional)*
½ cup	*Toasted and chopped hazelnuts*
For Creamy Coffee Filling	
200 gms	*Cream cheese, softened*
¼ cup	*Condensed milk*
1½ cups	*Whipping cream*
2 tbsps	*Coffee liqueur or strong coffee*
1 tsp	*Coffee essence*
For Espresso Sauce	
1 cup	*Hot water*
⅓ cup	*Instant coffee powder*
1 tin (400 gms)	*Condensed milk*
¼ cup	*Butter*

To Garnish

Whipped cream and chopped dark chocolate

METHOD

For Creamy Coffee Filling

Beat cream cheese and condensed milk in a large bowl with an electric beater until light and fluffy. Whip the cream separately until soft peaks form. Add whipped cream to cream cheese mixture. Beat until fluffy. Fold in the coffee liqueur or strong coffee and essence. Set aside.

For Espresso Sauce

Mix together hot water, coffee powder, condensed milk and coffee liqueur (if using) in a saucepan and bring to a boil gently. Remove from heat, add butter and mix well. Set aside.

To Assemble

Place one of the chocolate sponge at the bottom of an eight inch round glass dish. Brush the cake with liqueur (if using). Top it with one-third of the coffee filling. Drizzle one-third of espresso sauce over it. Sprinkle two tablespoons of hazelnuts. Repeat the layers twice more, ending with the cake layer. Cover and refrigerate for one-two hours. Garnish with whipped cream and chopped chocolate and serve cold.

Frozen Chocolate Mousse Squares

Makes 12 squares

INGREDIENTS

12 pieces	*Oreo cookies, crushed*
1 tbsp	*Melted butter*
200 gms	*Philadelphia cream cheese*
½ tin (200 gms)	*Condensed milk*
250 gms	*Dark cooking chocolate, melted*
1 cup	*Whipping cream*

To Garnish

Whipping cream, chocolate curls and chocolate syrup

METHOD

Mix melted butter and crushed cookies in a bowl and press them onto the bottom of nine inch square pan lined with greaseproof paper or foil. Beat cream cheese until smooth. Gradually add condensed milk and chocolate, mixing well after each addition. Fold in whipped cream. Stir gently until well blended. Spoon this mixture over the crust. Freeze for five hours or overnight. Remove from freezer 15 minutes before serving. Cut into one and a half x one and a half inches squares and place each one in a plate and garnish with chocolate curls and swirls of chocolate syrup around the squares.

Chocolate Fruit Towers

Serves 4-6

INGREDIENTS

For Chocolate Biscuits

1 cup	*Plain flour sieved with ½ tsp baking powder*
¼ cup (each)	*Icing sugar and butter*
½ cup	*Chopped dark chocolate, melted with 2 tbsps of cream*
200 gms	*Sliced fruit (strawberry, kiwi or peach)*

For Orange cream

200 gms	*Whipping cream*
2 tsps	*Grated orange rind*
2 tsps	*Orange liqueur or essence*
2 tbsps	*Powdered sugar*

For Chocolate sauce

1 cup	*Thick cream*
½ cup	*Dark cooking chocolate, melted*
1 tbsp	*Chocolate liqueur (optional)*

To Garnish

1 tbsp each of icing sugar and thick cream, 2-3 slices of fruit

METHOD

For the Biscuits: Sift the flour, baking powder and icing sugar into a bowl; stir in combined chocolate-cream mixture in two batches. Mix to a soft dough. Turn onto a floured surface and knead lightly until smooth. Cover and refrigerate for 15 minutes. Roll the pastry between greaseproof paper to three mm thickness. Cut nine cm rounds. Place them on greased baking trays and bake in moderate oven for 10 minutes. Cool on trays.

For Orange cream: Beat the cream in a small stainless steel bowl until firm peaks form; fold in rind and essence or liqueur. Refrigerate.

For Chocolate sauce: Combine cream, chocolate and liqueur (if using) in a small bowl, stir until smooth. Refrigerate until thick and pourable.

To Assemble: Pour chocolate sauce in a plate. Drop a tiny amount of cream on the edge of like plate. Draw a skewer through sauce and cream to create a heart shape. Place one biscuit over the sauce. Pipe orange cream onto the biscuit; top it with five-six pieces of fruit. Repeat layering with biscuits, orange cream and fruit. Dust the top with sifted icing sugar. Chill until ready to serve.

Chocolate Fruit Towers

Frozen Chocolate Mousse Squares

Tiramisu

Tiramisu

Serves 6-8

Tiramisu is a cool, refreshing Italian dessert that was initially created in Sienna, a northwestern province of Tuscany. The word Tiramisu means "pick me up." It is a very light mocha-flavored with whipped cream concoction of sheets of sponge cake soaked with strong coffee and a tantalizing hint of liqueur.

INGREDIENTS

250 gms	Mascarpone cheese
3	Egg yolks
2	Egg whites
6 tbsps	Sugar
⅓ cup	Marsala wine or sherry
½ cup	Fresh cream
¼ kg	Sponge cake, cut into sheets
2 tbsps	Kahlua
2 tsps	Camp coffee essence
½ cup	Strong coffee

To Garnish

Chocolate powder and grated chocolate

METHOD

Slice the sponge cake into thin sheets, toast them lightly and set aside. Make a zabaglione (basic custard, made with eggyolks, sugar and marsala wine) by beating the egg yolk and sugar in the top of a double boiler until it becomes ivory-coloured. Add Marsala and whisk over simmering water until the mixture begins to thicken. Allow it to cool slightly. Add one-fourth cup of coffee to mascarpone with three tablespoons of sugar. Beat it into the zabaglione mixture. Whip the cream to soft peaks and fold it into the zabaglione mixture gently. Beat the egg whites until stiff and fold into the mixture as well. Set aside till you assemble. Mix the remaining coffee with Kahlua and Camp coffee and soak the toasted sponge cake sheets with them. Line a big glass bowl or stemmed glasses for individual servings with the sponge cake sheets. Pour the zabaglione mixture over it to cover the whole cake till about half an inch high. Again layer the sponge cake sheets alternately with the mixture till the brim of the glass or bowl. Finish with cream on the top. Cover and freeze for six-eight hours. Just before serving, garnish with chocolate powder and shavings. Serve chilled.

Note: Zabaglione set in individual stemmed glasses is also served as an independent dessert.

Tiramisu (Eggless)

Serves 6-8

INGREDIENTS

200 gms	*Mascarpone cheese*
200 gms	*Whipping cream*
½ cup	*Powdered sugar*
½ cup	*Strong coffee*
250 gms	*Sponge cake, slice into thin sheets*
2 tbsps	*Coffee liqueur (Kahlua or Irish cream)(optional)*
2 tsps	*Camp coffee essence or vanilla essence*

To Garnish

Grated and powdered chocolate

METHOD

Whip the cream in a chilled stainless steel bowl with an electric beater. Mix Kahlua (if using), coffee or vanilla essence into the strong coffee. Combine Mascarpone, powdered sugar and beat for two minutes with the beater on medium speed. Then add one-fourth cup of coffee and continue beating. Do not over beat. Fold the whipped cream into the Mascarpone mixture. Take the toasted sponge cake sheets and soak them with the coffee mixture and line the serving bowl or individual glasses with them. Pour the Mascarpone mixture over it and alternate with soaked sponge sheets, the last layer being that of the cheese mixture. Refrigerate for four-six hours. Garnish with grated and powdered chocolate and serve chilled.

Mocha Tiramisu Trifle

Serves 8

INGREDIENTS

2 (250 gms)	*Chocolate sponge cakes*
1 tbsp	*Coffee liqueur (optional)*
½ cup	*Toasted and chopped hazelnuts*
For Creamy Coffee Filling	
200 gms	*Cream cheese, softened*
¼ cup	*Condensed milk*
1½-cups	*Whipping cream*
2 tbsps	*Coffee liqueur or strong coffee*
1 tsp	*Coffee essence*
For Espresso Sauce	
1cup	*Hot water*
⅓ cup	*Instant coffee powder*
1 tin (400 gms)	*Condensed milk*
¼ cup	*Butter*

To Garnish

Whipped cream and chopped dark chocolate

METHOD

For Creamy Coffee Filling

Beat cream cheese and condensed milk in a large bowl with an electric beater until light and fluffy. Whip the cream separately until soft peaks form. Add the whipped cream to cream cheese mixture. Beat until fluffy. Fold in the coffee liqueur or strong coffee and essence. Set aside.

For Espresso Sauce

Mix together hot water, coffee powder, condensed milk and coffee liqueur (if using) in a saucepan and bring to a boil gently. Remove from heat, add butter and mix well. Set aside.

To Assemble

Place one of the chocolate sponge at the bottom of an eight inch round glass dish. Brush the cake with liqueur (if using). Top it with one-third of the coffee filling. Drizzle one-third of espresso sauce over it. Sprinkle two tablespoons of hazelnuts. Repeat the layers twice more, ending with the cake layer. Cover and refrigerate for one-two hours. Garnish with whipped cream and chopped chocolate and serve cold.

Strawberry Tiramisu

Serves 6-8

INGREDIENTS

250 gms	*Mascarpone cheese*
1¼ cup	*Whipping cream*
500 gms	*Strawberries, washed, stemmed and quartered*
½ cup	*Powdered sugar*
1 tbsp	*Lemon juice*
1 tbsp	*Strawberry liqueur (optional)*
250 gms	*Sponge cake (recipe on page 20)*

To Garnish

Strawberries and whipped cream

METHOD

Slice the cake into thin sheets and toast them. Soften the Mascarpone cheese and whip the cream until soft peaks form. Fold it into the cheese. Sprinkle sugar over the strawberries and cook them slightly on a low flame. When liquid seeps out of the fruit, remove from the stove and cool. Add the lemon juice and liqueur. Drain out the juice from the strawberries in a small bowl. Place one cake sheet at the bottom of seven to eight inch sized transparent dish. Soak it with strawberry syrup. Spread the Mascarpone mixture over the cake evenly. Top it with strawberries. Repeat with soaked cake sheet, Mascarpone and the strawberries. Finish with a soaked cake sheet. Whip the cream to soft peaks. Spread a thin layer over the cake sheet. Cover and chill for two-four hours. Pipe the remaining cream around the border and arrange halved strawberries.

Kulfi Trifle
(Indian Ice-cream Trifle)

Serves 4-6

INGREDIENTS

200 gms	*Nut biscuits or sponge fingers*
200 gms	Malai Kulfi, *slightly softened*
1 cup	*Whipping cream*
1 cup	*Chopped fruit*
1 tsp	*Vanilla essence*
½ cup	*Chocolate sauce (optional)*
¼ cup	*Slivered almonds*

To Garnish

Whipped cream and sliced fruit

METHOD

Arrange biscuits or sponge fingers at the bottom of a medium sized bowl. Dribble half of the chocolate sauce all over the biscuits. Spread half of the soften *Kulfi* over the biscuits. Sprinkle half the almonds and half of the chopped fruit. Whip the cream with the vanilla essence until stiff. Set aside some for garnish. Spread half of the remaining cream evenly over the fruit. Repeat these layers once more. The top layer of the cream can be piped instead of spreading it. Cover and chill for two-three hours. Garnish with whipped cream and fruit slices just before serving.

Note: For individual servings, arrange the layers in six stemmed glasses instead of a bowl.

Coffee Brownie Trifle

Serves 8

INGREDIENTS

8 pieces	*Chocolate brownies (½"squares) (recipe on page 250)*
1 cup	*Strong Coffee*
200 gms	*Softened cream cheese*
½ cup	*Cold milk*
200 gms	*Dark cooking chocolate*
1 tbsp	*Coffee essence or Kahlua*
1 cup	*Whipping cream*
1 cup	*Sliced fruits*

To Garnish

Whipped cream and sliced fruits

METHOD

Cut brownies into half horizontally and soak with one-fourth cup of coffee. Beat the cream cheese and remaining coffee in a bowl until smooth. Melt chocolate with milk and cool. Whip the cream to form soft peaks, add the essence or Kahlua. Fold in cooled chocolate mixture into the cheese mixture and finally fold in the cream. Layer brownies, fruit and chocolate mixture in eight individual transparent glasses or six cup-sized glass bowl. Chill for two-three hours. Garnish with whipped cream and fruit slices.

Black Magic Torte

Serves 6

INGREDIENTS

24 pieces	*Oreo cookies*
1 tbsp	*Melted butter*
500 gms	*Chocolate ice cream*
250 gms	*Vanilla ice cream*
½ cup	*Whipping cream*

To Garnish

Chocolate fudge velvet sauce (recipe on page 24)

METHOD

Finely crush 14 cookies. Measure three-fourth cups of crumbs and mix them with one tablespoon of butter. Line a seven inch pie dish with this mixture. Halve the remaining cookies. Set aside four to six pieces and stand the remaining around the edge of the pie dish, pressing lightly into the crust. Scoop out chocolate ice cream from the box with an ice cream scoop and arrange over the prepared crust. Sprinkle four to six crushed cookies over this. Spread softened vanilla ice cream over the cookies. Smoothen the surface and freeze for 15 minutes. Sprinkle remaining cookie crumbs out of the first 14 cookies and press lightly into ice cream. Whip the cream to stiff peaks and pipe to decorate. Cover and freeze for several hours or overnight. Garnish with fudge sauce just before serving.

Kahlua Brownie Torte

Serves 6

INGREDIENTS

8 pieces	*Chocolate brownies, (1/4" ht) (recipe on page 250)*
2 tbsps	*Kahlua or any other coffee liqueur*
1 1/2 tsp	*Gelatine powder*
4 tbsps	*Water 125 gms cream cheese*
1/4 cup	*Icing sugar*
200 gms	*Fresh cream*
100 gms	*Dark cooking chocolate, melted*

To Garnish

Grated chocolate

100 gms fresh cream beaten with 2 tbsps of icing sugar

METHOD

Line the serving bowl with brownies and dribble kahlua all over. Set aside. Sprinkle gelatine over cold water in a small pan. Gently heat until the liquid is transparent. Cool at room temperature. Beat cream cheese in a bowl until smooth. Beat in icing sugar. Add cream, beat until just combined. Beat in gelatine mixture. Pour this in the serving bowl lined with brownies. Refrigerate for four-five hours or overnight. Pipe beaten cream and decorate with chocolate before serving.

White Chocolate and Strawberry Mousse Torte

Serves 10

INGREDIENTS

For the Crust

225 gms	*Chocolate wafer biscuits*
100 gms	*Melted butter*

For the Mousse

⅓ cup	*Strawberry liqueur or thin strawberry syrup*
1 ½ tsps	*Gelatine powder*
600 gms	*Strawberries, washed and stemmed*
½-¾ cup	*Powdered sugar*
300 gms	*White chocolate, cut into pieces*
2 cups	*Whipping cream*
¾ cup	*Powdered sugar*
1 tsp	*Vanilla essence*

To Garnish

2-3 whole strawberries and chocolate shavings

METHOD

For the Crust

Grind wafer biscuits in the food processor. Add butter and mix till crumbs are moist. Press mixture into a nine inch round loose bottom tin and freeze it.

For the Mousse

In a medium saucepan, sprinkle gelatine over the liqueur or the syrup and set aside for 20 minutes. Purée the strawberries, setting aside three-four whole ones. The strawberry pulp should measure one and two-third cups. If it is less, add more strawberry syrup. Add sugar and strawberry pulp to the gelatine mixture. Slowly heat until the sugar melts and the gelatine dissolves. Remove from stove and add white chocolate. Stir till melted. Transfer the mixture to a large bowl and chill over ice, stirring often. Make sure the mixture does not set. In a stainless steel bowl beat the cream with sugar and vanilla. Fold this into the strawberry mixture in three additions.

Pour over the prepared crust and smoothen the top. Freeze the torte till it sets for four-six hours. Cut around the edges of the pan and release from the sides. Transfer to a plate and garnish with halved strawberries and chocolate shavings.

Double Chocolate Hazelnut/ Almond Torte

Serves 6

INGREDIENTS

¾ cups	*Powdered sugar*
¾ cups	*Plain flour*
1 cup	*Ground hazelnuts/almonds*
½ cup	*Butter*
½ cup	*Cream*
125 gms	*Dark cooking chocolate, melted*
125 gms	*White cooking chocolate, melted*
400 ml	*Whipping cream*
2 tbsps	*Gelatine powder mixed with 3 tbsps of water*
2 tsps	*Vanilla essence OR*
2 tsps	*White rum*

To Garnish

Whipped cream, cracked toffee and chocolate curls

METHOD

Grease and line a nine inch loose bottom tin with grease proof paper. Grease the paper. The bases can be cooked one at a time. Beat butter and sugar together until fluffy. Add cream and beat again. Mix the flour and ground nuts together and fold them in gently into the butter-sugar mixture. Spread one-third of this mixture evenly on a prepared tin. Bake in a moderate oven for 25 minutes or until firm. Stand five minutes before removing from the base. Repeat the same for the remaining mixture. Melt gelatine over low heat until transparent. Whip the cream until thick. Place melted dark and white chocolate in two bowls. Fold in half the cream and one teaspoon of vanilla or rum to white chocolate. Add half of the gelatine mixture in a thin stream. Set aside. Repeat the same for the dark one. Place one hazelnut pastry at the bottom of a nine inch loose bottom tin. Spread the dark chocolate mixture evenly. Top it with another piece of pastry. Layer the white chocolate mixture followed by the remaining hazelnut pastry. Cover and freeze until set. Remove from pan and place it onto a serving plate. Garnish with whipped cream, cracked toffee and chocolate curls.

Death By Chocolate

Serves 10-12

INGREDIENTS

200 gms	*Almond meringues or macaroons, halved*
12-14 pieces	*Chocolate brownies*
3-4 tbsps	*Dark rum (optional)*

For Chocolate Ganache

250 gms	*Dark cooking chocolate, broken into pieces*
2 tbsps (each)	*Powdered sugar and butter*
1½ cups	*Fresh cream*

For Mocha Mousse

250 gms	*Dark cooking chocolate, broken into pieces*
3 tbsps	*Instant coffee*
¼ cup	*Water*
2 tbsps	*Cocoa powder*
1 cup	*Whipping cream*
3-4 tbsps	*Powdered sugar*

For Mocha Rum Sauce

2 tbsps (each)	*Hot water, instant coffee powder and coffee essence*
1 cup	*Chopped cooking chocolate*
½ cup	*Cream or milk*
1 tbsp	*Rum*

To Garnish

Chopped chocolate and whipped cream

METHOD

For Chocolate Ganache

Heat the cream and butter together on medium heat. Bring to a boil. Place chopped chocolate in a bowl and pour the cream over it. Allow it to stand for five minutes. Stir until smooth. Keep at room temperature until needed.

For Mocha Mousse

Place cooking chocolate, instant coffee, water and cocoa powder in a double boiler. Heat for five-seven minutes. Stir the mixture until smooth. Set aside to cool. Whip the cream with sugar in a stainless steel bowl to soft peaks. Fold in the cream little by little to cooled chocolate mixture. Refrigerate till ready to assemble.

For Mocha Rum Sauce

Combine all the ingredients in a saucepan and gently heat, stirring all the time. Set aside to cool.

To Assemble Death By Chocolate

Place half of the brownies, top side up, in a loose hot tin or a wide glass bowl. Dribble dark rum over them. Ladle one and a half cups of chocolate ganache over the brownies. Place halved meringues, broken side up, over ganache, pressing down gently to eliminate air pockets. Spoon the mocha mousse on top of the meringue, spreading evenly. Place remaining brownies, bottom side up on top of mocha mousse. Dribble dark rum if using. Chill for 30 minutes. Remove from the fridge and pour remaining ganache and freeze again until set. If you are using a loose hot tin, you may invert the cake on a platter or if setting in a bowl, freeze Death by chocolate for 4 to 12 hours. Garnish with whipped cream and chopped chocolate on top and serve with mocha sauce poured over each helping.

Ice Cream Truffles

Serves 8 (Makes 24)

INGREDIENTS

½ kg (each)	*Vanilla, coffee and chocolate ice cream*
500 gms	*Semisweet cooking chocolate, chopped*
1½ tbsps	*Salad oil*
1 cup (each)	*Sliced and toasted almonds and pistachios*
2 cups	*Chocolate vermicelli*

METHOD

Line a large baking sheet with waxed paper. Using one and a half inch round ice cream scoop, scoop out eight round balls of each vanilla, coffee and chocolate ice cream. Place them on a prepared sheet. Freeze ice cream overnight. Combine chopped chocolate and vegetable oil in large metal bowl. Place bowl over saucepan of simmering water. Alternately melt chocolate with oil in the microwave oven on high for one-two minutes. Stir until chocolate is smooth. Remove bowl from water. Cool chocolate until barely lukewarm. Place almonds, chocolate vermicelli and pistachios in three medium separate bowls. Line three flat plates with waxed paper. Working with one vanilla ice cream ball at a time and working quickly, drop into lukewarm melted chocolate. Using a fork, turn to coat and lift out chocolate-coated ball. Drop the ball off the fork into a bowl with almonds, using hands to turn to coat. Place truffle in a prepared pie dish. Repeat with remaining vanilla ice creams balls. Place them in the freezer. Follow the same procedure, dropping coffee ice cream balls into chocolate and then pistachios and chocolate ice cream balls into chocolate and then vermicelli. Freeze all the ice cream truffles for two hours, and then cover and keep them frozen. Place one of each type of ice cream balls into each serving bowl.

Peach Yogurt

Serves 2

INGREDIENTS

2 large	*Peaches, peeled and chopped*
Grated rind and juice of 1 orange	
1 cup	*Thick yogurt*
1-2 tbsps	*Icing sugar*
1 tsp	*Gelatine mixed with three tablespoons of water OR*
1	*Egg white*
A small pinch of cinnamon powder	

METHOD

Cook the gelatine mixture (if using) on a low heat till melted or stiffly beat the egg white. Set aside. Blanch and stone the peaches. Liquidize them with orange juice and the rind. Beat yogurt and cream with sugar. Fold in the peaches in yogurt mixture. Mix well. Add the gelatine mixture (if using) in a thin stream while beating or if using egg white fold them in now. Sprinkle cinnamon powder and mix well. Pour this in a pint-sized bowl and chill for two-three hours.

Note : Strawberries or ripe mangoes can be used instead of for peaches.

Chocolate Soup

Serves 4-6

INGREDIENTS

2 cups	*Light cream*
1½ tbsp	*Milk powder*
⅓ cup	*Sugar*
2 tbsps	*Cocoa powder*
2 tbsps	*Corn flour*
¼ cup	*Milk*
1 tsp	*Butter*
A pinch of salt	
½ tsp	*Vanilla essence*
1 tbsp	*Amaretto (almond liqueur) (optional)*

To Serve

Cinnamon toast

To garnish

Slivered and toasted almonds

METHOD

In a small saucepan mix together milk powder, sugar, cocoa, corn flour, butter and milk. Gently bring to a boil, stirring continuously. Add the cream and bring to a boil. Remove from heat and add vanilla and Amaretto (if using). Chill to serve cold or serve hot. Garnish with almonds and serve with cinnamon toast.

Note: You may add extra milk or cream to further thin the soup.

Frozen Mocha Almond Crumble

Serves 6-8

INGREDIENTS

50 gms	*Dark cooking chocolate*
2 tbsps	*Butter*
2 tbsps	*Sugar*
1 tbsp	*Instant coffee powder*
1 tbsp	*Camp coffee essence*
500 gms	*Coffee ice cream*
1 cup	*Slivered and toasted almonds*
100 gms (1/2 cup)	*Dark chocolate cookie crumbs*

To Garnish

Whipped cream and roasted coffee beans

METHOD

In a small saucepan, melt chocolate, butter and sugar together. Remove from stove and add instant coffee mixed with one-fourth cup of hot water and Camp coffee essence. Set aside to cool. Slightly soften the ice cream and layer half of it in a serving bowl. Swirl half the chocolate mixture followed by almonds and cookie crumbs over the ice cream in layers. Repeat the layers in the same order and garnish with whipped cream and coffee beans. Cover the bowl with cling wrap and freeze if until ready to serve.

Biscuit Tortoni

Serves 8

INGREDIENTS

½ cup	*Almonds, blanched, chopped and toasted*
150 gms	*Amaretti biscuits, cut into ½" pieces*
3 tbsps	*Dark rum or strong coffee*
½ cup	*Semi sweet chocolate pieces*
1 cup	*Whipping cream*
1 tsp	*Vanilla essence*
1 kg	*Vanilla ice cream, softened*

To Garnish

Whipped cream and slivered almonds

METHOD

Arrange cookies in medium bowl and sprinkle them with rum or coffee. Toss with almond and chocolate chips and set aside. In a large bowl, beat the cream with vanilla until soft peaks form. Spoon it over the cookie mixture. Fold in cookie and cream mixture into the ice cream and freeze until serving.

Garnish with whipped cream and slivered almonds and serve.

Plum and Custard Parfait

Serves 6

INGREDIENTS

For the plum mixture

500 gms	*Plums, pitted and sliced*
Grated rind and juice of 1 orange	
1/4 cup	*Sugar*
2 tbsps	*Corn flour*

For the custard

2 cups	*Milk*
3 tbsps	*Corn flour*
6 tbsps	*Sugar*
1 tsp	*Vanilla essence*
1/2 cup	*Whipping cream*
1/2 cup	*Thick cream*

To Garnish

Plum slices and sprigs of mint leaves

METHOD

For Plum Mixture

Put the plums in a heavy saucepan with sugar, orange rind and orange juice. Heat, stirring constantly. Cook until plums are tender. Remove from stove and cool slightly. Pass it through a sieve in a bowl and set aside to cool completely. Add the corn flour and gently boil until the mixture thickens.

For the Custard

Mix all the ingredients for the custard in a heavy saucepan, and heat gently until thick and lump free. Add the thick cream and set aside to cool. Whip the cream until double in quantity and fold it into the custard. In a stemmed glass, spoon alternate layers of plum puree and custard. Chill glasses for two-three hours until custard has set. Garnish with plum slices and fresh mint sprigs before serving.

Fruit Salsa Parfait

Serves 8

INGREDIENTS

For the Salsa

1 cup	*Pineapple chunks, tinned or fresh*
1½ cups	*Chopped peaches, tinned or fresh*
2 pieces	*Kiwi, peeled and cubed*
1 large	*Apple, peeled and cubed*
2-3 tbsps	*Powdered sugar*
2-3 tbsps	*Orange juice*
¼ tsp	*Powdered cinnamon*
¼ tsp	*Ground ginger*
1½ cups	*Whipping cream*
½ cup	*Praline powder (recipe on page 55)*

METHOD

Toss all the fruit, sugar, spices and orange juice in a medium bowl. Whip the cream until soft peaks form. Fold in the praline powder. Layer the fruit salsa and whipped cream alternately in eight dessert glasses. Chill and serve.

Drink Suggestion With This Dessert:

Tropical Punch Mock Margarita

Serves 6

INGREDIENTS

1½ cups	*Cold water*
1 cup	*Orange juice*
2 tbsps	*Lemon juice*
1 cup	*Tropical soft drink mix*
4 cups	*Ice cubes*

METHOD

Blend all the ingredients except ice in a blender jar until drink mix is dissolved. Add ice cubes and blend again. Pour it out in salt-rimmed glasses and serve with fruit salsa parfait.

Rasmalai Parfait

Serves 6

INGREDIENTS

6	*Cottage cheese balls in syrup (Rosogollas)(recipe on page 106)*
½ cup	*Crushed pistachios*
2	*Kiwi fruit, peeled and chopped*
1 cup	*Whipping or double cream*
¼ cup	*Icing sugar*
6	*Wafer sticks*

To Garnish

Sprigs of mint leaves

To Serve

6 stemmed glasses

METHOD

Remove cottage cheese balls from the syrup and cut each one into two. Whip the cream to soft peaks and beat in the icing sugar. Gently fold in the pistachios. Take stemmed glasses and place one halved cottage cheese ball at the bottom. Layer with pistachio cream and kiwi. Repeat the process once more. Layer all the glasses in the same way. Chill. Garnish with mint leaves and serve with wafer sticks.

Mango Parfait

Serves 6

INGREDIENTS

2 medium sized	*Alphonso mangoes, peeled and chopped*
½ cup	*Mango pulp*
2 tbsps	*Corn flour*
2 cups	*Milk*
½ cup	*Sugar*
½ tsp	*Lemon juice*
1½ tbsps	*Gelatine, mixed with ¼ cup of water*
¾ cup	*Fresh cream, beaten*

To garnish

A few chopped mango pieces

METHOD

In a medium saucepan, mix together milk, sugar and corn flour. Bring to a boil stirring all the time. Simmer and cook until thick. Remove from the stove and set aside to cool. In a small pan, heat the gelatine mixture until dissolved. Add lemon juice and cool. Beat this into the cooled milk along with the cream. Divide this mixture into two parts. Add mango pulp to one part and half of chopped mangoes to the other. Take individual stemmed glasses and layer both the custards alternately with mango pieces in between, to create three different layers. The top layer should be the chopped mango. Chill in the refrigerator for one-two hours before serving.

Butterscotch Praline Sundae

Serves 4-6

INGREDIENTS

For the Sundae

½ kg	*Vanilla ice cream*
½ kg	*Butterscotch ice cream*
1 cup	*Praline sauce*

For the Praline Sauce

¼ cup	*Butter*
½ cup	*Brown sugar*
2 tbsps	*Maple syrup or honey*
¼ cup	*Water*
1 tsp	*Rum or brandy (optional)*
½ cup	*Finely chopped nuts (almonds, walnuts, cashews, or a mixture of all three)*

METHOD

Semi soften both the ice creams in separate bowls and press down in the desired tin forming two layers (vanilla and butterscotch). Freeze overnight.

To make the sauce, heat the butter over medium heat until golden, and cool. Gradually add sugar, mixing until smooth. Stir in the syrup and water. Bring to a boil and stir for one minute. Cool slightly, then stir in the rum/brandy and nuts. When you want to serve, unmould the ice cream onto a serving plate, pour the warm sauce over it and serve. Alternately layer the ice-creams in individual stemmed glasses and pour the sauce over.

Orange, Chocolate, Mascarpone Cream Sundae

Serves 6

INGREDIENTS

For Chocolate-Mascarpone cream

150 gms	*Dark or white chocolate, coarsely chopped*
1½-cup	*Thick cream*
½ cup	*Mascarpone cheese*
1 tsp	*Vanilla essence*

For Orange Coulis

2½ cups	*Fresh orange juice*
½ cup	*Powdered sugar*
1 tbsp	*Grand Marnier*
1 tbsp	*Corn flour*

For Oranges

2 cups	*Orange segments*
1 tbsp	*Grand Marnier*
1 tsp	*Powdered sugar*

To Assemble

4-5 slices	*Sponge cake*

METHOD

For Chocolate Mascarpone Cream

Place chocolate in a medium-sized bowl. Gently boil the cream in a small saucepan. Remove from stove and pour over the chocolate. Let the mixture stand for 30 seconds to melt. Gently whisk until smooth. Beat in Mascarpone cheese and vanilla. Cover and refrigerate till cold.

For Orange Coulis

Combine orange juice, corn flour and sugar in a saucepan and cook over medium heat, stirring constantly with a wooden spoon, until the sugar is dissolved and the mixture thick. Strain the mixture through a sieve and add Grand Marnier. Cover and chill.

For the Oranges

Set aside a few whole slices of orange. Mix remaining segments with sugar and Grand Marnier and chill.

To Assemble

Cut the cake slices into one-fourth inch cubes. Divide them among six dessert glasses. Pour two tablespoons of coulis over cake cubes. Toss these cubes with a spoon in the orange coulis. Remove chocolate mixture from the refrigerator. Beat until soft peaks form. Fill the piping bag with a large star nozzle with this mixture and pipe some into each dessert glass. Top with orange segments and again pipe the chocolate mixture. Garnish with whole orange slice. Refrigerate till ready to serve.

Traditional English Trifle

Serves 8

INGREDIENTS

250 gms	*Plain sponge cake (recipe on page 20)*
3 tbsps	*Brandy*
6 tbsps	*Marsala wine*
1 small can	*Apricots*
½ cup	*Strawberry jam*
200 gms	*Whipping cream*
2 cups	*Classic English custard (recipe on page 23)*

To Garnish

Maraschino cherries, halved walnuts, whipped cream and grated chocolate

METHOD

Cut the sponge cake into half and then into half inch pieces. Mix brandy and Marsala wine in a cup. Drain the apricots and puree the fruit. Make the custard and cool to room temperature. Whip the cream until soft peaks form. Line the base of a transparent bowl with half of the cake pieces and soak them with half of brandy liquid. Spread half of apricot puree over cake pieces. Top it with half of strawberry jam. Spread custard and whipped cream on top of soaked cake evenly. Repeat the layers once more, finishing with cream layer. Garnish lavishly with whipped cream, walnuts, Maraschino cherries and grated chocolate. Cover and chill in the refrigerator for 4-6 hours.

Chocolate Paté

Makes 2 cups

INGREDIENTS

200 gms — *Bittersweet chocolate, finely chopped*
¾ cup — *Fresh cream*
¼ cup — *Finely ground hazelnuts*
A pinch of salt

To Serve

Slices of fresh fruit, sweet biscuits, sponge fingers

METHOD

Place chocolate and salt in a heat-proof bowl. In a small saucepan heat the cream gently, stirring occasionally just until it begins to boil. Remove from heat and add two-thirds of the cream and hazelnuts to the chocolate. Allow it to stand for two-three minutes. Stir very gently to melt. Gradually add the remaining cream. If the chocolate is not completely melted, keep over a pan of hot water until smooth. Cool the mixture briefly and then turn it out into a serving bowl and chill. Serve with fruits, sponge fingers and cookies.

Note: You may use 150 gms of bittersweet chocolate and 50 gms of milk chocolate for a sweeter Paté.

Shrikhand (Saffron-flavoured Yogurt)

Serves 2

INGREDIENTS

250 gms — *Plain yogurt*
3-4 tbsps — *Sugar or*
3 sachets — *Sugar substitute*
½ tsp — *Cardamom powder*
A few strands or saffron

To Garnish

Thinly sliced almonds and pistachios

METHOD

Tie the yogurt in a muslin cloth for one hour or till the all the water is drained out. Place it in a bowl and mix in the sugar. Sieve mixture to get a smooth consistency. Mix saffron threads in a little water and add this to the yogurt along with the cardamom powder. Mix well and transfer to a serving bowl. Sprinkle the nuts and chill in the refrigerator until ready to serve.

Chocolate Paté

Ice Cream Truffles

Navratna Rabri
Rosogollas
Sutarfeni Delight

Sutarfeni Delight
(Soft Vermicelli Sweet)

Serves 6-8

INGREDIENTS

250 gms x 2 circles	*Sutarfeni, white or with saffron (purchased)*
1 cup	*Cottage cheese, grated*
½ cup	*Icing sugar, sieved*
1 tsp	*Corn flour*
½ cup	*Fruit of your choice, freshly chopped (pineapple, orange, mango, chopped mixed dry fruits)*
¼ cup	*Sugar syrup*

To Garnish

A few rose petals and sliced fruit

METHOD

In a medium bowl, place cottage cheese, icing sugar and corn flour and mix well. Add finely chopped fruit of your choice to this mixture. Now place one of the sutarfeni bonds on a lightly-greased baking tray and heat slightly in a moderate oven, just to make it a little crisp. Remove from the oven and let it cool slightly. Place sutarfeni onto a serving dish and spread the cottage cheese mixture over this evenly. Make the other sutarfeni slightly crisp in the oven and place that over the cottage cheese mixture. Pour sugar syrup over the sutarfeni, making sure it does not leak out from the sides. Garnish with rose petals and fruit slices. Cut it into triangle pieces and serve at room temperature or cold.

Navratna Rabri (Thickened Milk with Fruits and Dry Fruits)

Serves 6

INGREDIENTS

1½ litre — *Milk*
8 tbsps — *Sugar*
A few strands saffron
½ tsp — *Cardamom powder*
½ cup — *Chopped dry fruit (almonds, cashew, pistachios, glace cherries and dates)*
¾ cup — *Chopped fresh fruit (apples. oranges and grapes)*

METHOD

Boil the milk on a low flame till reduced to half. Keep pushing the cream that forms on top to the side of the pan. Mix saffron in little milk and add it to the hot milk along with the sugar, cardamom powder and dry fruits. Cook for two-three minutes. Remove from heat and cool at room temperature. Add fresh fruits and mix well. Transfer to a serving dish and chill before serving.

Cold Cherry Soup

Serves 4

INGREDIENTS

450 gms — *Fresh cherries*
4 cups — *Water*
1 level tbsp — *Corn flour*
3 tbsps — *Sugar*
Lemon juice to taste
A little red wine (optional)
To Garnish
Mint leaves, whipped cream and few halved cherries

METHOD

Wash, stem and stone the cherries. Reserve a few for the garnish. Put the remainder of the cherries in a saucepan with the water and simmer until tender. Rub the fruit and water through a sieve and reheat to boiling point. Mix the corn flour and sugar with a little water, add to the soup and cook for 10 minutes. Add lemon juice and wine (if using) and chill. Garnish with cream, stoned cherries and mint leaves.

Strawberry-Angoor Rasmalai (Strawberry-flavoured milk with cottage cheese dumplings)

Serves 6-8

INGREDIENTS

1 litre	*Milk, boiled and reduced*
6 tbsps	*Sugar*
12-15 pieces	*Small cottage cheese dumplings (recipe on page 106)*
½ cup	*Sliced strawberries*
2 tbsps	*Sliced pistachios*

METHOD

Boil the milk on a slow flame until reduced to two-thirds. Add sugar and continue boiling to reduce further to half. Remove from stove and add cottage cheese dumplings and cool it in the refrigerator. When chilled, add sliced strawberries and chill again. Just before serving, garnish with pistachios.

Grape and Melon Delight

Serves 4-6

INGREDIENTS

1 medium	*Musk melon*
100 gms	*Grapes, red or green, chopped*
1 pkt.	*Lemon jelly*
½ cup	*Whipping cream*
1 tsp	*Lemon juice*

METHOD

Make the jelly and allow it to cool and begin to thicken. Add lemon juice. Cut the melon into a shape pf a basket. To do this, leave a strip along the top, as a handle, and cut all the pulp. Scoop center of the pulp and chop neatly. Mix diced melon and chopped grapes with most of the jelly. Keep aside some for garnish. Whip the cream until soft peaks form and fold it in the fruit mixture. Stuff the melon basket with this and spread remaining jelly over the top. Chill until set. Serve cold.

Chilled Fruit Soup

Serves 4

INGREDIENTS

1 large (each)	*Apple and pear, peeled and cubed*
2 tbsps	*Whole wheat flour*
¼ cup	*Orange juice*
2 tbsps	*Lemon juice*
1 tsp	*Grated rind of orange*
1 tsp	*Lemon*
1 medium	*Orange, peeled*

Sugar to taste

To Garnish

Thin slices of lemon and a few mint leaves

To serve

Stemmed dessert glasses and almond cookies

METHOD

Put apple and pear in water in a saucepan and bring to a boil. Add orange and lemon rind and simmer for 20 minutes. Remove from stove and rub through a sieve. Mix flour with four tablespoons of water and stir into the purée. Return to a pan and bring to a boil. Simmer the soup for five minutes. Allow it to cool slightly, add lemon and orange juice and sugar to taste. Chill in the refrigerator for two-three hours. Serve with an orange slice in each glass and garnish with mint leaves. Serve chilled in dessert glasses with almond cookies.

Lemon Snow Pudding

Serves 6

INGREDIENTS

2 tsps	*Gelatine powder*
¾ cup	*Sugar*
¾ cup	*Boiling water*
¼ cup	*Lemon juice*
1 tsp	*Grated lemon rind*
3	*Egg whites*
A pinch of salt	

METHOD

In a large bowl, sprinkle gelatine over half a cup of cold water to soften. Add half a cup of sugar, salt and boiling water. Stir to dissolve the gelatine. Add lemon juice and mix well. Cool over a bowl of ice until thick. Beat the egg whites until foamy. Gradually add remaining sugar, beating well after each addition. Beat the gelatine mixture until foamy. Gently fold in the egg whites into the gelatine mixture. Turn the mixture out onto four cup sized mould and refrigerate until firm. To unmould, run a spatula around the edge of the mould. Invert onto a serving plate. Shake the mould gently to release. Serve right away.

Mohlet Saung
(Iced Coconut Milk With Sago)

Serves 4

INGREDIENTS

1 cup	*Sago*
4 cups	*Chilled water*
4 cups	*Medium-thick coconut milk, chilled*
½ cup	*Water chestnuts, chopped*
Dash of rose syrup	
¼-½ cup	*Rock sugar, made into syrup with little water*
2-3	*Ice cubs*

METHOD

Wash and soak the sago for approximately one hour. Drain and put it in a large saucepan with three cups of water. Bring to the boil and simmer over moderate heat until the sago grains are clear. Remove from stove and add water chestnuts along with rose syrup for colour. Cool and chill. Put the sugar in a small pan with the remaining water and heat gently until the sugar has dissolved. Cool and strain the syrup. Put about four tablespoons of sago and two-three pieces of water chestnut onto a dessert bowl, add three tablespoons of syrup and mix well. Add two-three ice cubes in each bowl and top it up with coconut milk and stir. Serve immediately.

Chinese Fruit Bowl

Serves 8-10

INGREDIENTS

1 medium sized	*Pineapple, cut into wedges (4 cups)*
1 tin or 2 cups	*Shelled lychees*
2 medium	*Bananas, sliced diagonally (2")*
3 medium	*Oranges, peeled and sectioned*
2 cups	*Fresh strawberries, washed and halved*
Juice of 1 lemon	
3-4 tbsps	*Powdered sugar*
2 tbsps	*Finely chopped candied ginger*

METHOD

In a large serving bowl, gently toss all the fruits alongwith sugar, lemon juice and ginger. Cover and refrigerate until well chilled, approximately for two hours.

Note : You can add one-fourth cup of white rum to this fruit bowl.

Tricolour Ice-cream Bomb

Serves 12

INGREDIENTS

1½ litre	*Vanilla ice cream*
1 litre	*Chocolate ice cream*
1 cup	*Whipping cream*
2 tbsps	*Powdered sugar*
2 tbsps	*Copped glace cherries*
2 tbsps	*Candied peel*
1 tbsp	*Kirsch (cherry liqueur) (optional)*

METHOD

Line bottom and side of a eight cup sized mould with vanilla ice cream. Freeze until firm. Cover with a layer of chocolate ice cream and freeze until firm. Beat the cream with sugar and kirsch (if using), until stiff peaks form. Set aside some for garnish and add the remaining ingredients to the remaining cream. Spoon this mixture in the centre of the moulded and firmed ice-cream. Spread evenly to make a smooth layer. Cover and freeze over night until firm. To unmould, dip the mould in hot water for six to eight seconds and invert onto a serving plate. Garnish with reserved cream and serve.

Sitafal Basundi
(Custard Apple Dessert)

Serves 4-6

INGREDIENTS

1½ litres	*Full fat milk*
6 tbsps	*Sugar*
1 cup	*Custard apple pulp*

A pinch of cardamom powder

To Garnish

Toasted and sliced pistachios

METHOD

Heat the milk with sugar on a slow flame, stirring from time to time until the sugar has melted. Put it on medium heat and boil until it reduces to half. During this process, do not stir but scrape off the milk fat on the sides. Remove from heat and cool completely. Add the custard apple pulp and mix well. Chill for two hours. Garnish with pistachios and serve.

Note: Any other fruit can be used i.e. peach, mango, orange, kiwi, etc.

Phirni
(Milk and Almond Pudding)

Serves 4-6

INGREDIENTS

1 litre — *Milk*
12 pieces — *Almonds, soaked overnight and blanched*
2 tbsps — *Rice, soaked overnight*
1 cup — *Sugar*
A few strands saffron

To Garnish

A pinch of cardamom powder, sliced and toasted, pistachios and almonds

METHOD

Grind almonds and rice separately with little water to a smooth paste. Boil the milk on moderate heat for 30 minutes, stirring occasionally. Stir in the ground rice, almonds and sugar. Continue boiling for 10-15 minutes, until the pudding is thick enough to coat the spoon. Remove from heat and add the saffron mixed with little milk. Cool at room temperature. Pour it in an earthen pot and garnish with cardamom powder and chopped nuts. Chill for four hours, until it is thoroughly chilled and firm to touch.

Rosogollas
(Cottage Cheese Balls in Sugar Syrup)

Makes 16 Rosogollas

INGREDIENTS

2 litres	*Cow's milk (Bought on previous day and skimmed)*
Juice of 1½ lemon	
3 cups	*Sugar*
6 cups	*Water*
1-2 drops	*Rose essence*
2 trays	*Ice cubes*

METHOD

Bring milk to a boil and gradually add lemon juice. The milk will start curdling and the water will begin to separate. When the liquid turns greenish, remove from fire and strain through a muslin cloth, and pour extra tap water to drain out excess fat from the cottage cheese. Process the cottage cheese through a small blender to achieve a smooth texture. Add rose essence and divide in 14-16 small-sized balls. In a steel pressure cooker, mix sugar and water and bring it to a boil. Increase heat to high and drop cottage cheese balls over boiling syrup. Boil for five minutes and cover and cook further on a medium flame for 20 minutes without the whistle. Remove from gas, open the lid and add ice cubes immediately. Cool and refrigerate until ready to serve or serve warm.

Hot Desserts

"Life's a pudding full of plums." Puddings are described as a plethora of baked, steamed, broiled, flambéed desserts, and are life's truly "comforting" foods. They are perfect for chilly fall and winter evenings.

Molten Chocolate Cake

Serves 6-8

INGREDIENTS

For the Cake

1½ cups	Plain flour
3 tbsps	Cocoa powder
1 tsp	Baking powder
½ tsp	Baking soda
¼ tsp	Salt
1 cup	Powdered sugar
1 cup	Water
6 tbsps	Melted butter
1 tsp	Vanilla essence
1 tsp	Oil to grease and dust the tin
1 tbsp	Plain flour to grease and dust the tin

For the Syrup

½ cup	Sugar
⅓ cup	Water
50 gms	Bitter cooking chocolate

For Fudge Sauce

½ cup	Fresh cream
¼ cup	Powdered sugar
2 tsps	Corn flour mixed with 2 tsps of water
125 gms	Bitter cooking chocolate
2 tbsps	Brandy (optional)

To Serve

500 gms Vanilla ice cream

To Garnish

Toasted almond flakes

METHOD

For the Cake : Preheat the oven to 350°F. Grease and dust eight inch square or eight inch ring mould pan. Sieve the flour, sugar, cocoa, baking powder, soda and salt together in a bowl. Add water, butter and vanilla. Mix well. Pour the mixture and bake it in a preheated oven for 25 minutes. Make the syrup and the fudge sauce while the cake is baking. Remove and set aside to cool slightly and then invert onto a warmed plate.

For the Syrup: Mix sugar and water in a small saucepan and heat gently until sugar melts. Bring to a boil and simmer for three-four minutes. Add chopped chocolate and stir until completely melted. Set aside to cool. Makes one cup.

For Fudge Sauce: Combine cream and sugar in a saucepan, stir constantly over heat without boiling till sugar dissolves. Stir in corn flour and water mixture. Boil until the mixture thickens. Remove from heat and add chocolate and stir until smooth. Add brandy if using. Serve hot or warm. Makes one and a half cups

To Serve: Invert warm cake onto a serving plate. Pour the syrup all over the cake, very slowly. Each addition has to be absorbed before adding the next one. Scoop the ice-cream in the centre of the cake and pour the fudge sauce over the ice-cream. Sprinkle with almonds and serve immediately.

Note: If you wish to double the recipe, you will need a 13 inch x 9 inch pan.

Steamed Chocolate Pudding

Serves 6

INGREDIENTS

100 gms	*Dark cooking chocolate, broken into pieces and soften*
100 gms	*Butter*
4 large	*Eggs, separated*
100 gms	*Powdered sugar*
½ cup	*Plain flour, sieve before measuring*
⅔ cup	*Ground almonds*
⅔ cup	*Thick cream*
4-5 pieces	*Crumbled digestive or chocolate biscuits*

To Serve

Chocolate sauce (recipe on page 24)

METHOD

Butter a four cup pudding basin and dust it with sugar. Cream the butter and add softened chocolate, sugar and egg yolks. Continue beating until smooth. Whisk egg whites stiffly. Add remaining sugar and beat until well blended. Fold the egg whites into the creamed butter mixture with the flour, ground almonds and biscuit crumbs. Pour this into a prepared tin and steam for 30-45 minutes over simmering hot water or bake in a bain marie in a 180°c. oven. Test if pudding is baked with a skewer which should come out clean. Invert on a serving plate and serve hot with chocolate sauce around it.

Darsaan
(Honey-Coated Fried Noodles)

Serves 6

INGREDIENTS

For the Noodles

1 cup	*Plain flour*
3 tsps	*Oil*
½ tsp	*Salt*
A pinch of baking powder	
Oil	*For frying*

For the Sauce

2 tbsps	*Sugar*
2 tbsps	*Honey*

To Garnish

Almond flakes

To Serve

Vanilla or butterscotch ice cream

METHOD

Sieve the flour with baking powder and salt. Make a well in the centre and pour the oil. Mix it with your fingertips and make soft dough by adding cold water. Cover and set aside for half an hour. Roll out a nine inch round and roll it like a Swiss roll. Cut it at one cms interval and open up the strips. Fry them in hot oil.

While the noodles are frying, make the sauce. In a small saucepan mix together sugar with two tablespoons of water and heat on a slow flame. When the sugar melts, add the honey and mix well. Take it off the stove. Place fried noodles onto a serving dish and pour the honey sauce over them. Garnish with almond flakes and serve immediately with vanilla or butterscotch ice cream.

Sizzling Brownies (Eggless)

Serves 6-8

INGREDIENTS

For the Brownies

¼ cup	Powdered sugar
¼ cup	Brown sugar
1 cup	Plain flour, sieved
1 tsp (each)	Baking powder
1 tsp	Vanilla essence
½ tsp	Soda bi-carbonate
¼ tsp	Salt
3 tbsps	Cocoa powder
6 tbsps	Melted butter
1/3 cup	Chopped walnuts
1 tbsp	Vinegar
1 cup	Ice cold water

For the Sauce

¼ cup	Cocoa powder
¼ cup	Powdered sugar
2 tbsps	Butter
2 tbsps	Water
½ tsp	Vanilla essence

To Serve

Vanilla ice cream

METHOD

Sieve together plain flour, baking powder, soda, salt, powdered sugar and cocoa. Place this in a mixing bowl and add the remaining ingredients for the brownies. Mix well. Grease a 8 inch square tin and pour this mixture and bake in a hot oven at 350°F for 20-25 minutes. Remove and cool in the pan for 5-7 minutes. Cut into equal-sized squares and cool them on a wire rack. To make the sauce, mix all the ingredients together and heat through. Heat the sizzler plate thoroughly. Slightly brush it with oil. Just before serving, place two-three brownies on the plate, put a scoop of vanilla ice cream on each one. Bring this to the table immediately and pour boiling sauce over the ice-cream. The sauce, when poured over the plate should emit a sizzling sound. Make sure that the sizzler plate and the sauce are very hot!

Note: You may use chocolate fudge brownie recipe for the brownies with egg on page 250

Sizzling Brownies

Apple Fritters with Lemon Sauce

Date and Almond Wonton

Date and Almond Wontons

Makes 20 wontons

INGREDIENTS

20	*Wonton wrappers*
2 tbsps	*Powdered sugar*
1 tbsp	*Cinnamon powder*
1/4 cup	*Milk*
For frying	*Oil*
For the filling	
1/2 cup	*Finely chopped dates*
1/2 cup	*Brown sugar*
2-3 tbsps	*Toasted sesame seeds*
2-3 tbsps	*Chopped almonds*
1 tbsp	*Butter*
To Serve	
Vanilla ice-cream	

METHOD

For the filling

Slightly crush the sesame seeds and mix them with dates, sugar, almonds and butter. Set aside. Place one teaspoon of filling in the centre of a wonton wrapper. Lift up the opposite edges and stick them together with the help of milk and bring the corners together to form a hat-shaped wonton. Repeat this for the rest of the wontons and deep fry in oil until golden. Drain on a kitchen paper. Sprinkle a little of the sugar mixed with cinnamon powder on each one and serve hot with vanilla ice-cream.

Apple Fritters with Lemon Sauce

Makes 1 cup

INGREDIENTS

For the fritters

$1\frac{1}{2}$ cups	*Plain flour*
1/8 tsp	*Salt*
$1\frac{1}{4}$ tsps	*Baking powder*
1 large	*Egg or*
1 tbsp	*Corn flour mixed with $\frac{1}{3}$ cup of water*
2 tbsps	*Melted butter*
3 medium	*Apples, peeled and sliced*
Powdered sugar to sprinkle	
Oil	*For frying*

For Lemon Sauce

1 cup	*Sugar*
1 tbsp	*Butter*
3-4 tbsps	*Lemon juice*
1 tbsp	*Corn flour*
$\frac{1}{4}$ cup	*Water*

METHOD

For the Fritters

Mix the first five ingredients in a food processor until they crumble. Spoon the mixture into a large bowl. Immerse two to three slices of apple in the batter at a time. Coat them well with the batter and fry them in hot oil, in batches, two minutes on each side or until golden brown. Drain on kitchen paper. Sprinkle fritters with powdered sugar. Serve hot with lemon sauce.

Makes 20 fritters

For Lemon Sauce

Mix all the ingredients in a saucepan and cook over a medium heat, whisking constantly. Cook until thick. Serve hot.

Chocolate Waffles

Makes 4 waffles

INGREDIENTS

½ cup	*Butter*
1½ cups	*Plain flour*
1 cup	*Sugar*
1 tsp	*Baking powder*
¼ tsp	*Salt*
2 squares	*Chocolate, melted over hot water*
½ cup	*Milk*
2	*Eggs, separated*
½ tsp	*Vanilla*

To Serve

Hot maple syrup or whipped cream or ice cream.

METHOD

Cream the butter and sugar. Add well-beaten egg yolks and melted chocolate. Mix thoroughly. Sift the measured flour with baking powder and salt. Add this dry mixture alternately with milk to the chocolate mixture. Add vanilla and fold in stiffly-beaten egg whites. Bake in a hot waffle iron for eight-ten minutes. Serve with hot maple syrup, cream or ice cream.

Mocha Mystery

Serves 6

INGREDIENTS

3/4 cup	*Powdered sugar*
1 cup	*Sifted plain flour*
2 tsps	*Baking powder*
A pinch of salt	
1/4 cup	*Chopped cooking chocolate*
2 tbsps	*Butter*
1/2 cup	*Milk*
1 tsp	*Vanilla essence*
1/2 cup	*Brown sugar*
4 tbsps	*Cocoa powder*
1/2 cup	*Powdered sugar*
1 cup	*Strong coffee*

To Serve

Whipped cream and vanilla ice-cream

METHOD

Sieve plain flour, baking powder, salt and powdered sugar in a bowl. Melt butter and chocolate in a small pan and add to the dry mixture. Combine milk and vanilla essence and add to the flour mixture. Pour this into six individual pans or one square pan. In a small bowl, mix both the sugars and cocoa powder and sprinkle all over the flour batter. Pour cooled coffee over it and bake for 30-35 minutes at 150° C or 350° F. Remove from the oven and cool slightly. Cut into squares and serve with whipped cream or ice-cream.

Baked Chocolate Pudding (eggless)

Serves 4

INGREDIENTS

⅓ cup	*Plain flour sieved with a pinch of salt*
¾ tsp	*Baking powder*
1+½ tbsp	*Cocoa powder*
½ cup	*Powdered sugar*
¼ cup	*Milk*
1 tbsp	*Melted butter*
½ cup	*Chopped almonds*
½ tsp	*Vanilla essence*
½ cup	*Brown sugar*
1 cup	*Boiling water*

8 x 8 square baking tin, greased

To Serve

Vanilla ice cream or sweetened whipped cream

METHOD

Sieve the flour, baking powder, one tablespoon of cocoa and powdered sugar in a bowl. Add melted butter, milk and vanilla. Gently fold in the nuts. Pour this mixture in a prepared tin. Mix brown sugar and half a tablespoon of cocoa together and sprinkle over the pudding and set aside. Half an hour before you want to serve, preheat the oven to 400° F. Keep the boiling water ready boiling and pour it over the pudding. Bake in the oven for 25 minutes. The water will go through the cake mixture and will form like a thick sauce and settle at the bottom. While serving scoop a piece of pudding and pour the sauce from the bottom on each serving. Serve hot with vanilla ice cream.

Cappuccino Fondue

Serves 6-8

INGREDIENTS

1 cup	*Strong coffee*
½ cup	*Condensed milk*
½ cup	*Thick cream*
1 tsp	*Camp coffee essence*
1 tsp	*Corn flour*
1 tbsp	*Kahlua (optional)*
2-3 tbsps	*Sugar*

Milk to froth

To Garnish

Cinnamon powder

To Serve

Sponge fingers or chocolate wafer sticks

METHOD

Mix together strong coffee, condensed milk, thick cream, sugar and corn flour in a saucepan. Slowly heat until the mixture is thick. Remove from stove and add Camp coffee essence and Kahlua. Transfer this to a dessert fondue dish or a ceramic serving dish. Keep it simmering during serving. Heat the milk and beat it with the beater to create foam. Spoon the foam onto the simmering fondue and sprinkle cinnamon powder. The fondue should be simmering gently throughout. Serve with sponge fingers and chocolate wafers.

Hot Cherry Fondue

Makes 2 cups

INGREDIENTS

450 gms	*Fresh cherries, stemmed, stoned and halved*
½-¾-cup	*Sugar*
¼ cup	*Water*
2 tbsps	*Butter*
2 tbsps	*Corn flour*
¼ cup	*Lemon juice*
1 tsp	*Grated lemon rind*
1 tbsp	*Cherry liqueur (optional)*

To Serve

Sponge fingers or waffle pieces

METHOD

Mix together cherries, sugar and water in a saucepan. Cook until cherries are soft but firm. Remove from the stove and set aside to cool. Melt butter in a fondue dish over low heat; add cooked cherries with one-fourth cup of syrup. Mix corn flour with remaining cherry syrup and combine it with lemon juice. Mix well and add it to the cherry mixture. Add lemon rind. Cook until the mixture thickens. Add the liqueur (if using). Sponge fingers or waffle pieces.

You can use this as a topping for ice cream or a cake.

Strawberry Fondue

Serves 6

INGREDIENTS

450 gms	*Strawberries*
½ cup	*Powdered sugar*
2 tbsps	*Corn flour mixed with ¼ cup water*
1 tbsp	*Lemon juice*
1 tsp	*Strawberry essence or liqueur*
1 cup	*Thick cream*

To Serve

Sponge fingers or strawberry-flavoured wafer biscuits

METHOD

Wash and stem the strawberries. Soak them in cold water for 10-15 minutes. Puree them in a liquidizer and pass through a sieve. The puree should make two cups. In a small saucepan, mix the puree, sugar, lemon juice and corn flour mixture. Bring to a boil, stirring constantly. Cook until thick. Remove from stove and cool. Add the essence or the liqueur and the cream. When you want to serve, gently heat the mixture and transfer it to a fondue dish. Serve with sponge fingers or wafer biscuits.

Praline Fondue

Serves 4

INGREDIENTS

½ cup	*Sugar*
½ cup	*Chopped almonds*
100 gms	*White chocolate*
⅔ cup	*Fresh cream*
½ tsp	*Vanilla essence or brandy*

To Serve

Sponge cake cubes and fresh fruit pieces

METHOD

To make the praline, combine sugar and almonds in a heavy saucepan over medium heat. Stir from time to time. Cook until sugar turns golden brown. Pour this mixture onto an oiled baking sheet and set aside to cool for 15-20 minutes. Coarsely grind the nuts in a food processor. Put chocolate pieces and cream into a fondue pot and heat gently till the chocolate melts, stirring all the time. Add praline and vanilla or brandy. Mix well. Serve hot with cake cubes and fresh fruit pieces.

Note : You may add little milk if the mixture thickens while boiling.

Strawberry Waffles

Serves 6

INGREDIENTS

1 cup	*Plain flour, sieved*
2 tbsps	*Sugar*
1 cup	*Sliced strawberries*
4 tbsps	*Melted butter*
½ cup	*Milk*
¼ cup	*Thick cream*

Additional butter to grease the iron

To Serve

Strawberry sauce

METHOD

Place strawberries and sugar in a saucepan and cook until strawberries are slightly soft. Remove from the stove and set aside to cool. Mix with milk, cream and butter in a blender and process until smooth. Add pureed strawberry mixture to the flour, stirring until just moist.

Coat waffle iron with melted butter and preheat the iron. Spoon one-fourth cup of batter per waffle. Spread batter to the edge. Cook for 5-6 minutes. Serve hot with warm strawberry sauce.

Strawberry Sauce

In a medium saucepan combine one-fourth cup of sugar, three tablespoons of water, one tablespoon of strawberry jam. Stir over medium heat until sugar is dissolved. Mix one tablespoon of lemon juice with half tablespoon of corn flour; add it to sugar mixture. Cook till slightly thickened. Mix in one cup of sliced strawberries; heat through but do not overcook. Serve warm with waffles.

Makes 1 cup

Flambéed Strawberries with Vanilla Ice-Cream

Serves 6

INGREDIENTS

1 kg	*Vanilla ice cream quantity*
500 gms	*Medium sized strawberries, washed with the stems removed*
2 tsps	*Lemon juice*
5-6 tbsps	*Powdered sugar*
4 tbsps	*Orange juice (optional)*
2 tsps	*Butter*
¼ cup	*Brandy*
2 tsps	*Strawberry liqueur (optional)*

METHOD

Soak the strawberries in orange juice, lemon juice, strawberry liqueur and sugar for about half an hour. When you want to serve, place a small burner on the table. Heat a frying pan, melt the butter and add the strawberries soaked in juice. Let them cook until semi-soft. Pour brandy in a ladle and heat on the burner till the brandy catches the flame. Pour this over the strawberries and serve immediately with vanilla ice-cream.

Apple Strawberry Casserole

Serves 8-10

INGREDIENTS

3 cups	*Chopped apples*
2 cups	*Chopped strawberries*
1 ½ cups	*Sugar*
½ cup	*Butter*
½ cup (each)	*Rolled oats, plain flour and powdered brown sugar*
¼ cup	*Chopped nuts*

A pinch of salt and cinnamon

To serve

Cinnamon ice-cream

METHOD

Combine apples, strawberries and sugar in a large bowl and mix well. Place in a greased baking dish. Melt the butter in a small pan over low heat. Remove from stove and stir in oats, brown sugar, flour, cinnamon and salt. Stir until blended. Pour this mixture over fruit, spreading well to cover. Top with almonds. Bake at 150°C for 35-40 minutes or until the top is brown. Serve hot with cinnamon ice cream.

Strawberry Palmiers

Serves 6-8

INGREDIENTS

For the Base

10	Puff pastry biscuits (khari biscuits)
1/4 cup	Powdered sugar
1/2 tsp	Cinnamon

For the cream filling

2 cups	Milk
8 tbsps	Condensed milk
1/4 tsp	Salt
100 gms	Fresh cream or packet cream
1/4 cup	Plain flour
1 1/2 tsps	Vanilla essence
2 cups	Strawberries, sliced
1/4 cup	Powdered sugar

To Garnish

A few strawberries, halved

METHOD

Divide each biscuit into half. Place them in a baking dish and sprinkle sugar and cinnamon over it. Heat it in the oven at 150°C or 350°F for five minutes. Remove from the oven and let it cool.

For the Cream Filling

In a saucepan mix one and a half cups of milk, condensed milk and sugar. In the remaining half cup of milk, mix the plain flour and add to the boiling mixture. Stir continuously. Add the cream when it is thick. Take it off the stove, add vanilla and cool. When it is cooled, mix the sliced strawberries. Spoon this mixture over the biscuits and chill. Garnish with strawberries.

Note: As a variation, fresh mangoes or peaches can be used in place of strawberries.

In place of puff pastry biscuits, 200 gms of puff pastry can be used. In which case roll out the pastry and cook until crisp.

Churros
(Spiced Mexican Fritters)

Makes 16

INGREDIENTS

¼ cup	*Butter*
⅔ cup	*Plain flour, sifted*
2 large	*Eggs, beaten*
1 tbsp	*Ground almonds*
For frying	*Oil*

To Sprinkle

Icing sugar mixed with cinnamon powder and fruit sauce

METHOD

Place butter and two-third cup of water in a saucepan and heat gently, until the butter melts. Bring to a boil and while boiling, add the flour all at once and turn off the heat. Beat vigourously until mixture leaves the sides of the pan and forms a ball. Cool slightly, then beat in the eggs a little at a time, then add almonds. Spoon cooled mixture into a piping bag fitted with a large star nozzle. Heat the oil for frying till fumes come out. Pipe out three to four, two inch length fritters at a time into hot oil, cutting off the raw mixture with a knife. Dry them on towels and sprinkle sugar mixture. Serve hot by themselves or with fruit sauce.

Steamed Date and Almond Pudding

Serves 6

INGREDIENTS

1 cup	*Sliced dates*
1 cup	*Boiling water*
1½ cups	*Plain flour (sifted)*
1 tsp	*Soda*
½ tsp	*Baking powder*
½ tsp	*Salt*
2 tsps	*Butter*
1 cup	*Brown sugar*
¾ cup	*Almonds, toasted and chopped*
3-4 tbsps	*Milk*
1 tsp	*Vanilla essence*

To Serve

Warm custard or sweetend cream

METHOD

Pour water over dates and set aside. Sift together flour, soda, baking powder and salt. Grease a four cup sized mould with little butter. Keep four to five cups of water to boil in a steamer. Beat butter and sugar until creamy and fluffy. Add milk and vanilla essence to it. Fold in dry ingredients, dates mixture and almonds, and pour this mixture in the prepared mould. Cover with greaseproof paper and steam for 45 minutes. Remove from the stove and let it cool for 10 minutes. Invert on a serving plate and serve hot with warm custard or sweetened cream.

Note : Toasted and chopped walnuts can be used in place of almonds.

Crêpes Suzette

Serves 6-8

INGREDIENTS

1 recipe	*Basic sweet crêpes (recipe follows page no. 19)*
5-6 cubes	*Sugar*
2	*Medium oranges, washed*
100 gms	*Butter*
3 tbsps	*Grand Mariner (orange liqueur)*
2/3 cup	*Fresh orange juice*
1/2 cup	*Castor sugar*
3 tbsps	*Brandy*

METHOD

Make the sweet crêpes as per directions and set aside, covered, to avoid drying. To make orange butter, rub the sugar cubes over the oranges to extract the zest from the rind. Crush the cubes in a bowl with the back of a wooden spoon. With a small sharp knife, peel the oranges. Discard the white pith on the inside of the rind. Chop the rind very finely and add it to the bowl with the mashed sugar cubes. Add half the castor sugar and butter. With the back of a wooden spoon, cream the butter, sugar and rind together until light and fluffy. Work in four tablespoons of orange juice and the Grand Mariner and beat until the mixture is creamy. In a small frying pan, melt the orange butter over a low flame. Holding the outer edges of the crêpe with your fingertips, dip it into the heated butter mixture until well soaked. Carefully fold the crêpe in half, and then fold it again into a quarter. Transfer it to a shallow serving dish. Repeat the process with the remaining crêpes until they are all coated. Add the remaining sugar and orange juice to the remaining butter mixture and pour this over the crêpes. In a rounded metal spoon, heat the brandy over a low flame. Do not let it boil. Flambé this over the crêpes. When the flame dies down, serve with vanilla ice cream.

Crêpe Suzette

Chocolate Fondue

Fruit Kababs

Chocolate Fondue

Makes 3 cups

INGREDIENTS

6 oz or 150 gms	*Unsweetened chocolate or Toblerone chocolate*
1 cup	*Fresh cream*
1½ cups	*Powered sugar*
½ cup	*Butter*
3 tbsps	*Crème de cacao or Milk or Orange juice*

A small pinch of salt

For Dipping

Sponge cake pieces
Whole strawberries
Apple cubes
Banana slices
Orange sections

METHOD

Place the chocolate pieces in the upper vessel of a double boiler and melt it over hot water. Stir in the sugar, butter and salt. Stir until smooth. Beat the cream separately and add to the chocolate mixture. Stir in the liqueur. Pour into fondue pot and let it simmer over the burner. Serve with pieces of cake and fruits of your choice with long fondue forks or skewers.

Fruit Kababs

Serves 4-6

INGREDIENTS

1 cup	*Pineapple chunks*
12-14 pieces	*Strawberries, washed*
2-3 pieces	*Kiwi fruits, cubed*
2 large	*Bananas, cut into ½ " cubes*

Butter to grease the grill or frying pan

For Orange Baste

½ cup	*Orange juice*
2 tsps	*Lemon juice*
3 tbsps	*Honey or sugar*
2 tbsps	*Brandy (optional)*

A pinch of cinnamon

To Serve

Ice cream of your choice

METHOD

Make the baste by combining all the ingredients and place it in a wide bowl. Thread all the fruits onto the skewers. Brush them with baste. Set aside for half an hour. Barbecue the fruits, turning them from time to time and brushing them with baste. Serve hot with ice cream of your choice.

Date and Almond Cake

Serves 6

INGREDIENTS

1 cup	*Finely chopped black dates*
1 cup	*Boiling water + milk*
1½ cups	*Plain flour (sifted)*
1 tsp	*Soda*
½ tsp	*Baking powder,*
½ tsp	*Cinnamon powder*
½ tsp	*Salt*
½ cup	*Butter,*
½ tsp	*Powdered sugar*
½ tsp	*Brown sugar*
¾ cup	*Almonds, toasted and chopped*
1 tsp	*Vanilla essence*

To Serve

Warm custard or sweetened cream

METHOD

Pour water and milk over dates and set aside. Sift together flour, soda, cinnamon, baking powder and salt. Grease a six to seven inch cake tin and set aside. Beat butter and sugar until creamy and light. Add vanilla essence. Fold in flour mixture, soaked dates mixture and almonds. Pour it in the prepared tin. Bake at 350°F for 25-30 minutes. Remove from oven and let it cool for ten minutes. Invert on a serving plate and serve hot with warm custard or sweetened fresh cream.

Date and Almond Baklava

Makes 8

INGREDIENTS

500 gms	*Puff pastry*
1/4 cup	*Butter*
1/4 cup	*Milk*
1/4 cup	*Toasted*
1/4 cup	*Chopped almonds*
1/4 cup	*Sugar*
3/4 cup	*Finely chopped dates*

Little flour for rolling

To garnish

Toasted slivered almonds and powdered sugar

METHOD

Preheat the oven to moderate 180°C. Combine dates, sugar and milk in a saucepan and gently heat the mixture. Cook until liquid dries out. Remove from stove and add the almonds. Set aside to cool. Roll out the dough into a large square with the help of a little flour. Cut each one into 3 x 3 square. Brush each one with a little butter. Place one square on top of the other, overlapping at angles. Press them into small muffin cups or a cup cake tin. Repeat this for the rest of the pastry. When all the cups are made, spoon one tablespoon of date mixture in each one and make a parcel by joining the opposite ends and sealing the pastry. Lightly brush each baklava with little butter. Bake them in the hot oven for 35-40 minutes or until they are golden. Remove from the oven and cool slightly. Sprinkle them with powdered sugar and slivered almonds. Serve hot or cold.

Date Pancakes

Serves 6

INGREDIENTS

For the Pancakes

1 cup (each)	*Plain flour and water*
½ tsp	*Baking powder*
¼ tsp	*Salt*
2 tbsps	*Melted butter*

Butter to grease the pan

For the Filling

200 gms	*Dates, finely chopped*
1 tbsp	*Butter*
¼ cup (each)	*Powdered sugar and ground almonds*
½ cup	*Milk*
Oil	*For frying*

To Garnish

1 tbsp	*Toasted sesame seeds*

To Serve

Vanilla ice cream

METHOD

For the Pancakes

Sieve plain flour, baking powder and salt together in a bowl. Make a smooth batter with water and melted butter. Set aside for half an hour. To make the pancakes, pour one big spoon of batter onto a greased non-stick frying pan and shake the pan to spread the mixture in an even circle. Cook on both sides until slightly golden. Repeat for the remaining batter. Pile these pancakes on a plate, cover and set aside.

For the Filling

Melt butter in a small saucepan. Stir in dates, sugar and milk. Cook until the mixture leaves the sides of the pan. Remove from heat and add vanilla essence. Cool the mixture completely.

Before serving, heat the oil for frying. Place the pancake on a board and spoon one tablespoon of the date filling on each and fold into a cylindrical shape and seal the edges by using little bit of the mixture. Dab some sesame seeds on each one and deep fry in hot oil until crisp. Remove and drain on kitchen paper, cut into two and serve hot with vanilla ice cream.

Apple Jalousie

Serves 4-6

INGREDIENTS

4 cups	*Thinly sliced golden apples*
2 tbsps	*Lemon juice*
1 tsp	*Cinnamon powder*
2-3 tbsps	*Raisins*
1 tbsp	*Butter*
1 cup	*Powdered sugar*
1 tbsp	*Plain flour*
½ cup	*Water*
100 gms	*Puff pastry*
2 tbsps	*Apricot jam or orange marmalade*

Powdered sugar to sprinkle

To Serve

Whipped cream or vanilla ice cream

METHOD

Preheat the oven to 350°F. Grease a eight-nine inch pie dish with butter. In a bowl, toss together sliced apples, lemon juice, cinnamon powder, raisins, powdered sugar and plain flour. Spread evenly on a greased pie dish. Roll out the pastry to fit the pie dish. Slightly thin the marmalade or jam by adding little water and apply on-rolled pastry. Cover the top with this, marmalade side down. Slightly brush the top with butter. Bake in hot oven for 20 minutes. Remove from the oven and sprinkle sugar on top and serve hot with cream or ice cream.

Apple Crumble

Serves 4

INGREDIENTS

4 cups	*Thinly-sliced golden apples*
2 tbsps	*Lemon juice*
1 tsp	*Cinnamon powder*
2-3 tbsps	*Raisins*
⅓ cup	*Butter*
1 cup	*Powdered sugar*
¾ cup	*Plain flour*
½ cup	*Water*

A pinch of salt

A little butter to grease the dish

To Serve

Vanilla ice cream

METHOD

Preheat the oven to 350° F or 150°C. Grease one eight x eight inch-sized baking dish with a little butter. Toss apples with lemon juice, raisins and cinnamon powder. Arrange them on the baking dish. Pour water all around the apples. Mix together the flour, salt and sugar. Sprinkle all over the apples. Dot with butter. Bake it in a hot oven for 30 minutes or until the top is golden and crisp. Serve hot with vanilla ice cream.

Peach And Apple Cobbler

INGREDIENTS

1 kg	Ripe peaches
1	Large apples
½ cup	Sugar
½ cup	Cinnamon
2 tbsps	Plain flour
1 tbsp	Lemon juice
For the Topping	
1 cup	Plain flour
1 tsp	Baking powder
¼ tsp	Salt
½ tsp	Vanilla
4 tbsps	Butter
3 tbsps	Cream

A pinch of soda

1 egg or 3 tbsps of condensed milk

To Serve

Vanilla ice cream

METHOD

Peel and slice the peaches and apples. Combine with sugar and lemon juice. Mix the flour and cinnamon together and toss it into the fruit. Set this mixture aside in a saucepan.

For the Topping

Combine all the dry ingredients, cut the butter into small cubes and rub these cubes into the flour until they resemble breadcrumbs. Mix together the cream, vanilla and egg or condensed milk and pour this liquid into the dry ingredients. Mix everything together with a fork. With the help of a little flour on your palms, make circles which are two and a half inches in diameter and half inch in thickness. Preheat the oven to 400°F. Take an eight cup capacity baking dish. Heat the apple and peach mixture until the juices begin to boil. Pour this mixture into a baking dish and lay the rounds over the surface. Sprinkle a little sugar on top and bake until brown. Remove from the oven and let it rest for five minutes. Serve immediately with vanilla ice cream.

Toffee Apple

Serves 4-6

INGREDIENTS

1	*Golden apple*
1 tbsp	*Lemon juice*
½ cup	*Plain flour*
2 tbsps	*Corn flour*
¾ tsp	*Baking powder*
Oil	*For frying*

For the Caramel Coating

1 cup	*Sugar*
2 tbsps	*Oil*
2 tbsps	*Sesame seeds*

To Serve

A bowl with ice cubes and water and vanilla ice cream

METHOD

Peel, core and chop the apples into one inch by one inch cubes. Coat them with lemon juice and set aside. In another bowl, mix together plain flour, corn flour and baking powder. Add enough water to make a thick and smooth batter. Set aside. Make the caramel coating as given below. When ready, coat the apple pieces with this mixture and deep fry in hot oil until golden. Put the fried apples in the caramel coating evenly. Drain well and immediately drop them into the ice-cube bowl. Roll them till the caramel hardens. Drain and serve at once with vanilla ice cream.

For Caramel Coating

Place sugar, oil and two-third cup of water in a saucepan and cook on a high flame, shaking the pan from time to time to prevent it from burning. Cook until syrup turns light brown. Remove from the stove, add sesame seeds and mix well. Set aside.

Banana Fritters

Serves 6

INGREDIENTS

4	*Bananas, slit vertically*
For the Batter	
¼ cup	*Plain flour*
¼ cup	*Rice flour*
1 tsp	*Salt and*
1 tsp	*Sugar*
1 tsp	*Baking powder*
½ cup	*Milk*
Oil	*For deep-frying*
To Garnish	
1 tbsp	*Powdered sugar*
To Serve	
Coconut ice cream	

METHOD

Mix all the ingredients for the batter. Make a smooth paste. Set aside for half an hour. Dip the banana halves in the batter and deep fry in oil until golden. Remove and drain slightly and then dip them in powdered sugar. Serve hot with ice cream.

Steamed Ginger Pudding With Orange Sauce

Serves 4-6

INGREDIENTS

¾ cup	*Plain flour, sieved*
1 tsp	*Baking powder*
2 tbsps	*Grated ginger*
½ tsp	*Soda*
⅓ cup	*Butter*
⅓ cup	*Powdered sugar*
½ cup	*Milk*
For Orange Sauce	
1 cup	*Orange juice*
1 tbsp	*Orange rind*
2 tbsps	*Corn flour*
½ cup	*Sugar*

METHOD

Sieve the flour, baking powder and soda together. Toss ginger with the sieved flour. Set aside. Beat butter and sugar together until fluffy. Fold in the flour mixture and milk alternately. Spoon this mixture in a greased mould and cover with greaseproof paper. Steam for 45 minutes to one hour.

For Orange Sauce

Mix all the ingredients together in a saucepan and gently heat until thick. Turn the pudding out onto a serving plate and serve hot with orange sauce.

Baked Alaska

Serves 10-12

INGREDIENTS

1 9"x12"	*Rectangular sponge cake (made from basic sponge recipe on page 20)*
500 gms block	*Vanilla ice cream, frozen*
1 tin (500 gms)	*Peaches, drained and sliced*
½ cup	*Orange liqueur, Grand Marnier or Cointreau*
For the Meringue	
4-5 (120-150 gms)	*Egg whites*
½ tsp	*Cream of tartar*
A pinch of salt	
140-175 gms (each)	*Powdered sugar and icing sugar*
To Serve	
½ cup	*Cognac (to flambé)*

METHOD

Cut cooled sponge into two pieces vertically. Soak each piece with peach syrup. Place one part on the the ovenproof dish. Cut the ice cream block into two horizontal slices. Place one on the centre of the sponge, leaving the edges free. Cover with the other sponge and top it with remaining block of ice cream. Garnish the ice cream and the edge of the sponge with prepared and drained peaches. Pour the liqueur of the peach over the sponge. Place it in the freezer compartment of the fridge to keep the ice cream firm. Preheat the oven to 250°C 10-15 minutes before serving.

In a dry stainless steel bowl beat the egg whites with salt and cream of tartar until stiff. Gradually start adding powdered sugar, continuing to beat until stiff meringue is obtained and all the sugar is absorbed. Use a rubber spatula and gently fold in the icing sugar using an up and down movement. Cover and decorate the top and sides of the sponge with meringue using a piping bag with a star nozzle. Place at the top of very hot oven for 8-10 minutes. The meringue must turn light brown. Watch it all the time as it burns quickly. Take the dessert out of the oven and set a light to the cognac in front of the guests. And pour over the baked Alaska. Serve immediately.

Bread and Butter Pudding

Serves 4-6

INGREDIENTS

1/4 cup	*Butter*
6 slices	*Bread, crust removed*
1/4 cup	*Seedless raisins*
1 1/4 cup	*Milk*
1/3 cup	*Light cream*
3 tbsps	*Castor sugar*
2 large	*Eggs, beaten OR*
1/2 cup	*Thick cream mixed with 1 tsp corn flour*
1/2 tsp	*Vanilla essence*
A pinch of nutmeg	

METHOD

Grease a shallow baking dish with little butter. Preheat the oven to 180°C or 350°F. Spread the remaining butter on the slices of bread and cut them into triangles. Arrange them in layers, buttered side up, in the dish. Scatter raisins over the top. In a saucepan mix cream, milk and sugar. Heat gently until sugar melts. Do not allow the mixture to boil. Whisk the eggs and vanilla together and add to the cream mixture. Mix well. Pour over the bread through a sieve. Soak for one hour. Sprinkle the surface with nutmegs and place the dish over a shallow tin filled with water. Place this in a preheated oven and bake for 30-40 minutes, until set and golden brown. Cut into even sized pieces and serve hot.

Jalebi
(Pretzel-Shaped Sweet)

Serves 6-8

INGREDIENTS

2 cups	*Plain flour (maida)*
1 ½ cups	*Plain Yogurt*
½ cup	*Warm water*
3 tbsps	*Hot ghee*
½ kg	*Sugar*
1 tsp	*Cardamom powder*
1 tsp	*Saffron (powdered)*
Ghee for frying	
To Garnish	
3-4 tbsps	*Almonds and pistachios, sliced*
A few rose petals	

METHOD

Soak the flour in the yogurt, warm water and three tablespoons of hot ghee. Beat this mixture vigorously so that it is lump free. Cover and keep this vessel in a warm place. If the weather is cold you need to do this two nights before. Make one strand syrup from sugar, using just enough water. Add cardamom and saffron powder and keep it warm on a slow fire. Before serving, heat the ghee for frying in a broad vessel. Beat the *jalebi* mixture to a dropping consistency. Fill a cylindrical bottle with a small spout with this mixture. Form spiral-shaped rounds over hot ghee, about four-five *jalebies* at a time. Turn them over after using tongs. When they are golden, remove and soak them in hot syrup. Let them soak for five-seven minutes and remove on a serving plate. Garnish with almonds, pistachios and rose petals and serve at once.

Note : To powder saffron, heat a metal spoon and drop a few strands of saffron and allow them to dry completely. Powder them by crushing with back of the spoon.

Gajar Halva
(Carrot Sweet)

Serves 6-8

INGREDIENTS

500 gms	*Carrots, scraped and coarsely grated*
3 cups	*Milk*
1 cup	*Sugar*
3 tbsps	*Clarified butter*
½ cup	*Blanched*
½ cup	*Chopped almonds*
½ cup	*Cream*
½ tsp	*Cardamom seeds, powdered*

To Garnish

Slivered and toasted almonds and pistachios and edible silver leaf

METHOD

Put the carrots, milk and cream in a thick saucepan. Bring to a boil over high heat, stirring constantly. Continue cooking till the mixture is reduced to half its volume. Stir in sugar and continue cooking for 10 more minutes. Reduce the heat to the lowest possible point, add ghee and almonds. Cook further until the mixture is thick enough to draw away from sides of the pan. Remove from heat and add cardamom. Spread the prepared halva on a large serving dish and decorate with nuts and silver leaf. Serve warm or at room temperature.

Malpua
(Fried Pancake in Syrup)

Serves 6

INGREDIENTS

1 litre	*Milk, boiled and reduced to half*	
2-3 tbsps	*Plain flour*	|
¼ tsp	*Baking powder*	| *sieve together*
2 tbsp	*Powdered sugar*	|
250 gms	*Whole sugar*	
2-3 tbsps	*Thinly-sliced pistachios and almonds*	

A few threads of saffron
A pinch of cardamom powder
Ghee for frying

METHOD

Mix milk and plain flour mixed with baking powder and two tablespoons of sugar. Cover and set aside. Mix remaining sugar with water and boil to make a thick syrup. Add saffron and cardamom powder and keep warm in a serving dish. While frying the pancake, if you feel the batter is too thin, add a little more flour to gain thick pouring consistency. In a small frying pan, add one tablespoon of ghee and pour one dessert spoon of the flour-milk mixture and cook till golden. Turn over and cook the other side as well. Fold over to make half-moon shape. Place on a serving plate over the syrup. Repeat till all the pancakes are done. Sprinkle with chopped pistachios and almonds. Serve hot.

Note: To make orange malpua, mix a little orange juice along with water to make the syrup and add grated orange rind instead of saffron and cardamom. Also add half a teaspoon of orange essence to the batter.

Pastries and Pies

If elegance is your entertaining goal, try melting in the mouth piecrusts, a perfect blend of butter, flour and sugar, jeweled by attractive fruits and ultra rich flavours.

Brownie Mousse Pie

INGREDIENTS

For the Brownie Base

2 medium	*Eggs*
½ cup (each)	*Powdered sugar, brown sugar, butter and plain flour*
5 tbsps	*Cocoa powder*
¼ tsp	*Salt*
1 tsp	*Vanilla essence*
½ tsp	*Baking soda*
½ cup	*Finely chopped walnuts*

For the Mousse

200 gms	*Toblerone bar*
¼ cups	*Sugar*
¼ cup	*Fresh cream*
⅔ cup	*Whipping cream*
½ tsp	*Vanilla essence*

To Garnish

Whipped cream and chocolate shavings

To serve

Ice cream or whipped cream

METHOD

For the Brownie Base

Lightly grease an eight inch pie dish. Pre heat oven to 175°C. In a medium bowl, beat sugar and butter until light and fluffy. Add eggs, one at a time. Continue beating for one minute. Sift together flour, cocoa, salt and baking powder. Fold the flour mixture to the egg mixture very gently. Stir in the vanilla and nuts. Pour it into the prepared pie dish. Bake for 20-25 minutes. Remove and set aside to cool.

For the Mousse

Combine chocolate with sugar and one-fourth cup of cream in a bowl and melt over boiling water. Stir until completely melted. Add the vanilla essence and set aside to cool. Beat the cream over ice until stiff. Fold in to the chocolate mixture. Pour this over cooled brownie pie and garnish with whipped cream and chocolate shavings. Chill. Cut into wedges and serve with ice cream or cream.

Walnut-Chocolate Pie

Serves 8

INGREDIENTS

1 cup	Toasted and halved walnuts
1 cup	Thick cream
¾ cup	Sugar
½ cup	Brown sugar
½ cup	Butter
¼ cup	Melted cooking chocolate
¼ cup	Chocolate shavings
1 round 8"	Baked pie shell
½ cup	Water mixed with 2 tbsps of corn flour
½ tsp	Vanilla essence
A pinch of salt	

METHOD

In a double boiler top, beat brown sugar and butter until blended. Add sugar, salt, corn flour mixture and half a cup of cream. Mix well. Cook over boiling water, stirring for five minutes. Remove from water and stir in one cup of walnut and vanilla.

Melt the chocolate with half a cup of cream and brush the base of the pie shell with this. Pour walnut mixture over this and spread evenly. Bake for 30 minutes. Cool. Serve at room temperature.

Chocolate Marble Cheese Pie

Serves 6-8

INGREDIENTS

For the Crust

1½ cups	*Biscuit crumbs*
¼ cup	*Cocoa powder*
¼ cup	*Powdered sugar*
3-4 tbsps	*Melted butter*

For the Filling

⅔ cup	*Condensed milk*
360 gms	*Cream cheese*
2 tsps	*Vanilla essence*
1-cup	*Whipping cream*
¼ cup	*Cocoa powder*
1 tsp	*Vanilla essence*
2 tbsps	*Chocolate or coffee liqueur (optional)*

To Garnish

Chocolate curls

METHOD

For the Crust

In a medium bowl, stir together all the ingredients for the crust and press it down on the bottom and sides of a nine inch pie dish. Refrigerate for two hours before filling.

For the Filling

In a small saucepan, stir together cocoa and condensed milk. Cook over low heat, stirring constantly. Cook until thick. Remove and add one teaspoon of vanilla essence. In a small bowl, beat 180 gms cream cheese over ice, until light and fluffy. Add the cocoa mixture. Set aside. Whip the cream with one teaspoon of vanilla essence until thick. In a larger bowl, beat remaining cream cheese until light and fluffy. Fold in the cream, vanilla essence and liqueur (if using). Alternately spoon vanilla and chocolate mixtures into prepared crust. Gently swirl with knife or spatula for marbled effect. Refrigerate until set. Garnish with chocolate curls.

Brownie Pie

INGREDIENTS

2	Eggs or
4 tbsps	Condensed milk
1 tsp	Baking powder
1 cup	Sugar
½ cup	Butter, melted
½ cup	Plain flour, sieved
5 tbsps	Cocoa powder
¼ tsp	Salt
1 tsp	Vanilla essence
½ tsp	Baking soda
½ cup	Finely chopped walnuts

To Serve

Ice cream or whipped cream

METHOD

Lightly grease an eight inch pie dish. Pre heat the oven to 350° F or 175°C in a medium bowl, mix eggs with sugar and melted butter (if using condensed milk, reduce the sugar by two tablespoons). Sift together flour, cocoa, salt and baking powder (if making without eggs, sieve baking powder with the flour). Add the flour mixture to the egg mixture very gently. Stir in the vanilla and nuts. Pour it into the prepared pie dish. Bake for 20-25 minutes. Cool before cutting into wedges. Serve plain, with ice cream or with whipped cream.

Georgia Peach Pie

INGREDIENTS

For the Crust

2 cups	*Plain flour, sieved*
¾ cup	*Butter*
¼ tsp	*Salt*

For the Filling

8 pieces	*Peaches, peeled and sliced*	
½ cup	*Sugar*	*OR*
800 gms	*Tinned peaches, drained*	
¼ cup	*Sugar*	
¼ cup	*Plain flour*	
2 tbsps	*Lemon juice*	
½ tsp	*Cinnamon powder*	
1 tsp	*Grated rind of lemon*	
2 tbsps	*Milk*	

METHOD

For the Pastry

In a large bowl, combine flour and salt. Cut in butter until mixture resembles breadcrumbs. Sprinkle five to six tablespoons of cold water and toss it with fork to blend lightly. When the mixture forms a ball, knead gently. Divide the dough into two parts. Roll out one part into a 12 inch circle and press this into a nine inch pie dish. Let the extra pastry overhang. Roll out the remaining dough to 12" again and cut into half inch wide stripes. Set aside. Preheat the oven to 375°F.

For the Filling

If using fresh peaches, slightly stew them with little water. In a large bowl combine peaches, sugar, cinnamon, flour, lemon juice and grated peel. Toss well. Pour filling into prepared crust. Arrange reserved strips in a lattice pattern over the filling. Trim strips to match the lower part of the crust overhang. Dampen the exposed dough slightly and seal. Flute the edge decoratively. Brush lattice with milk and bake for 50 minutes, until bubbling with a golden crust. Remove, and cool slightly before serving.

Tarte Tatin
(Caramelized Apple Tart)

Serves 6-8

INGREDIENTS

For the Pastry

½ cup	*Plain flour*
¼ cup	*Butter, at room temperature*
A pinch of salt	

For the Filling

900 gms	*Dessert apples, peeled, cored and thinly sliced*
Juice of 1 lemon	
½ cup	*Brown sugar*
1 tsp	*Powdered cinnamon*

8" inch tin brushed with melted butter and lined with grease proof paper

To Serve

Whipped fresh cream or ice cream

METHOD

Preheat oven to 350°F (180°C). Sift the flour with salt in a bowl. Cut the butter into small cubes and rub into the flour with fingertips. The mixture should resemble breadcrumbs. Add one tablespoon of ice-cold water and bring together the dough to form a smooth ball. Add more water if needed. Wrap this in a polythene bag or foil and place in the freezer for 10 minutes before rolling out. Cover the base of the greased tin with brown sugar, pressing it down evenly. Sprinkle cinnamon. Toss apples with lemon juice and arrange neatly over sugar. Roll out the pastry dough to half inch thickness and cut out a circle that will fit the top of the tin. Cover the apples with the pastry, pressing it down gently. Place in the centre of the oven and bake for 40 minutes until the pastry is golden. When the tart is quite cold, loosen it round the edges, cover with a serving plate and turn it upside down. Remove paper and serve with fresh cream or ice cream.

Georgia Peach Pie

Tarte Tatin

Lemon Meringue Pie

Lemon Meringue Pie

Serves 8-10

INGREDIENTS

For the Pastry

100 gms	Butter, melted and lukewarm	
200 gms	Plain flour	Sieve together
½ tsp	Salt	
1 tbsp	Powdered sugar	
Grated rind of 1 lemon		Beat together
1 tbsp	Fresh cream	
1	Egg	

For the Filling

Juice of 5 lemons	
4 level tbsps	Plain flour
2 level tbsps	Corn flour
¾ cups	Water
240 gms	Powdered sugar
4	Egg yolks
1 tbsp	Butter

For the Meringue

3	Egg whites
100 gms	Icing sugar
2 tbsps	Lemon juice or one tablespoon of juice and one tablespoon of lemon essence
A pinch of salt	
A pinch of cream of tartar	

To Serve

Vanilla ice cream or Whipped cream

METHOD

For the Pastry

Preheat the oven to 180°C. Place the flour mixture in a bowl, make a well in the centre. Add the butter and rub in using fingertips. When the mixture resembles breadcrumbs, add the egg and cream mixture and make a soft dough. Cover it and chill in the fridge for an hour. Remove and roll out the pastry very lightly to fit in a ten inch pie dish. Prick it with a fork and bake blindly for 25 minutes on the middle rack until the pastry is golden.

For the Filling

To make lemon curd, mix together the flour, corn flour, water and lemon juice, beating with a whisk. Gradually bring it to a boil, beating all the time. Add sugar gradually and continue beating. Remove from the heat. Cool slightly. Beat together egg yolks and butter. Add to the lukewarm mixture and whisk until it becomes thicker. Set aside to cool.

Remove the pastry from the oven, but leave the oven on at 180°C. Pour lemon cream over the pastry and set aside.

For the Meringue

Beat to gather egg whites cream of tartar and salt, starting slowly and gradually increasing the speed. Once the mixture is stiff, add sugar slowly, a spoon at a time, till all the sugar is incorporated. Add essence or lemon juice and fold in gently with a spatula. Place in a piping bag and decorate the pie. Cook on the middle rack of the oven for approximately 10 minutes until the meringue is light brown. Serve at room temperature with whipped cream or vanilla ice cream.

Grape Quiche

Serves 6-8

INGREDIENTS

For the Pastry

200 gms	*Plain flour, sieved with ½ tsp salt*
100 gms	*Cold butter*
2 tbsps	*Powdered sugar*
Grated rind of lemon	
2 tbsps	*Cold water and*
2 tbsps	*Cream*

For the Filling

700 gms	*Fresh grapes, washed, dried and stems removed*	
⅔ cup	*Ground almonds*	*Mix in a bowl*
1½ tbsps (each)	*Lemon juice and sugar*	
2 tsps	*Orange Marmalade*	
1 cup (each)	*Milk and whipped cream*	
3 tbsps (each)	*Corn flour and powdered sugar*	
1 tsp	*Vanilla essence*	

To Garnish

Whipped cream

METHOD

For the Pastry

In a bowl, mix together the flour, powdered sugar and lemon rind. Rub in the butter to resemble breadcrumbs. Add cream and cold water to bind soft dough. Cover and refrigerate to firm. Remove from fridge and turn it out on a floured surface. Roll a nine inch round three mm thick pastry. Fit it in a shallow pie dish. (8" round) Prick it with a fork. Bake it in a hot oven for 15 minutes or until golden brown. Set aside to cool. Apply the almond and marmalade mixture to the bottom of the pastry to seal the crust.

For the Filling

Mix milk, sugar and corn flour in a saucepan and gently heat. Remove when translucent and thick. Cool. Add the cream and the vanilla. Pour this mixture over the glazed pastry. Spread evenly. Arrange the grapes standing up close to each other. Pipe the whipped cream in between the grapes. Chill. Cut into wedges and serve.

Ice Cream Pie with Mocha Fudge Sauce

Serves 8

INGREDIENTS

1 litre	*Butterscotch ice-cream*
For the crust	
2 tbsps	*Melted butter*
2 tbsps	*Sugar*
½ tsp	*Cinnamon powder*
⅓ cup	*Sliced nuts*
⅔ cup	*Vanilla wafer cookie crumbs*
For Mocha Sauce	
2 tbsps (each)	*Cocoa powder, butter and boiling water*
1 cup	*Whipping cream*
1 cup	*Sugar*
1 tbsp	*Instant coffee powder*
¼ cup	*Water mixed with one tbsp of corn flour*
¼ cup	*Chopped dark chocolate*
1½ tbsps	*Coffee or vanilla essence*

To Garnish

Whipped cream and slivered almonds

METHOD

Mix all the ingredients for the crust and press it down in a nine inch pie dish and set aside. Slightly soften the ice cream and spread over the crust. Smoothen the top, cover and chill for three-four hours or over night.

For the Sauce

Stir two tablespoons of boiling water and coffee powder in small bowl until coffee is dissolved. Whisk sugar and cocoa in heavy medium saucepan. Whisk in one cup of cream, corn flour mixture, and coffee powder. Add chocolate and butter. Bring to a boil over high flame, stirring constantly. Reduce heat to medium and simmer until slightly thickened, stirring occasionally for about four minutes. Cool for 30 minutes. Stir in coffee or vanilla essence.

Garnish ice-cream pie with whipped cream and slivered almonds and serve with the sauce.

White Chocolate Fruit Tart

Serves 10-12

INGREDIENTS

For the Tart

¾ cup	Butter
½ cup	Sugar
1½ cups	Plain flour, sieved

For the Filling

350 gms	White chocolate, chopped
¼ cup	Thick cream
200 gms	Cream cheese

For the Topping

2 cups	Assorted fresh fruit, sliced
¼ cup	Sugar
1 tbsp (each)	Corn flour and lemon juice
½ cup	Pineapple juice

To Garnish

A sprig of mint leaves and whipped cream

METHOD

For the Tart

Preheat the oven to 300°F. In a small mixer bowl, beat butter and sugar until smooth. Blend in the flour. Form a soft ball and press this down and sides of a 12 inches pie dish. Trim the edges. Bake for 20-25 minutes in the oven. Remove and set aside to cool.

For the Filling

Melt the chocolate and cream together over medium heat. Beat until smooth. Remove and cool. Beat the cream cheese and fold in the cooled chocolate mixture. If the mixture feels a little dry, add little milk. Set aside.

For the Topping

In a small saucepan, stir together sugar, corn flour and the juices. Cook over a medium heat, stirring constantly, until thickened. Cool.

To Assemble

Spread the chocolate filling evenly over the baked tart. Arrange sliced fruit on top. Carefully pour or brush the juice mixture over the fruit. Refrigerate until ready to serve. Garnish with mint and whipped cream.

Chocolate Fruit Tart

Serves 8

INGREDIENTS

For the Pastry

2 cups	*Plain flour, sieved*
3 tbsps	*Cocoa*
3 tbsps	*Powdered sugar*
1 cup	*Chilled butter*
6 tbsps	*Cold water*

For the Filling

1 cup	*Whipping cream*
1 cup	*Sliced fruit of your choice*
3 tbsps	*Jam or marmalade mixed with 2 tbsps of water*
1 tsp	*Fruit liqueur of your choice (optional)*

METHOD

For the Pastry

Sift the flour, cocoa and sugar together. Cut the butter into small chunks and add to the flour mixture, rubbing with your fingertips until it resembles breadcrumbs. Add cold water until pastry begins to form a ball. Roll it to form a circle, cover and chill in the refrigerator for 30 minutes. Press it into nine inch round tart case or eight small three inches cases. Bake at 180° C or 360° F for 20 minutes. Remove from the tins to cool.

For the Filling

Whip the cream until soft peaks are formed. Add liqueur (it using). Spoon enough cream to cover the bottom of the pastry and smoothen it. Arrange fruit of your choice. Mix jam or marmalade with water and heat slightly. Cover the fruit with one tablespoon of this syrup and chill for half an hour or serve right away.

Chocolate Mille Feuille

Serves 8-10

INGREDIENTS

250 gms	*Puff pastry dough (ready made)*
Butter to brush the pastry	
200 gms	*Bittersweet chocolate*
2 cups	*Milk*
3 tbsps	*Corn flour*
2½ tbsps	*Butter*
1 cup	*Whipping cream*
1 tsp	*Vanilla essence*

To Garnish

Icing sugar and chocolate shavings

METHOD

Mix milk, sugar and corn flour in a saucepan and bring to a boil stirring continuously. Stir in the chocolate and butter, and then remove from stove. Transfer this into a bowl and place this over a bowl of ice water. Stir frequently until smooth and cool. Whip the cream until it holds soft peaks. Set aside some for the top to garnish. Gently fold in the remaining cream into the prepared pastry cream.

Cut the dough into two parts and roll out each one individually to nine into four inches rectangles. Place them on a greased baking tray side by side. Brush lightly with butter and make the marking on each one to avoid rising. Bake in a hot oven at 375°F for 10-15 minutes or until golden colour. Remove and set aside to cool. Place one part on an oblong serving tray; spread half of the chocolate pastry cream evenly. Cover with the other pastry and pipe the remaining chocolate as well as the plain cream alternately. Generously sprinkle sugar all over the dessert. Garnish with chocolate shavings. Chill until ready to serve.

Miniature Mud Pie With Chocolate Sauce

Makes 12 tarts

INGREDIENTS

500 gms	*Roasted almond ice cream*
For the Tart Shells	
1 cup	*Butter*
3 tbsps (each)	*Cocoa powder and powdered sugar*
2 cups	*Plain flour, sieved*
5-6 tbsps	*Cold water*
For Bittersweet Chocolate Sauce	
¼ cup (each)	*Water and sugar*
1 cup (each)	*Dark cooking chocolate and thick cream*
To Garnish	
Sliced fruit	

METHOD

For the Tart Shells

Sieve together flour, cocoa powder and sugar in a bowl. Cut butter into small cubes and rub in with your fingertips to resemble breadcrumbs. Add cold water to form a ball. Cover and refrigerate for 30 minutes. Roll out the dough into a big circle and cut four inches rounds to fit a three inch pie shell. Trim excess dough.

Preheat the oven to 350°F. Arrange them on a baking tray and chill for 20 minutes. Bake for 12-14 minutes. Remove from oven, Cool the tarts on a wire rack. Remove from pie shell.

For Bittersweet Chocolate Sauce

Combine water and sugar in a saucepan, bring to a boil and cook until sugar dissolves. Melt chocolate in a microwave or in a double boiler. Add sugar syrup when the chocolate has melted. Boil the cream separately and pour into the chocolate mixture and stir until smooth and shiny. Cool at room temperature.

When ready to serve, place each tart shell on a serving plate. Put a scoop of ice cream onto each one. Pour or drizzle cooled chocolate sauce over the tarts covering them completely. Serve at once.

Pineapple Squares

Makes 60 squares

INGREDIENTS

500 gms	*Plain flour (sifted)*
1 tsp	*Salt*
400 gms	*Cold butter, cut into cubes*
1 cup	*Sour cream mixed together*
1 tbsp	*Sugar mixed together*
1 tsp	*Lemon essence*
750 gms	*Freshly chopped pineapple*
150 gms	*Sugar*
3 tbsps	*Corn flour*
12"x16"	*Rectangular baking tray*

A little icing sugar to sprinkle

METHOD

Place flour, salt and butter in a bowl. Mix in using two forks. Add sour cream-sugar mixture and lemon essence to the flour. Mix well with a wooden spoon. Leave the dough to stiffen in the freezer for 30 minutes. Drain the pineapple and mix with sugar and corn flour in a saucepan. Cook gently until the mixture becomes clear and thick. Set aside to cool. Divide the pastry into two parts. Roll out both halves. Line the baking tray with one of the halves. Pour the cooled pineapple mixture over it and spread evenly. Cover with the other half of the pastry. Put it in the freezer for 15 minutes till firm. Pre-heat the oven to 180°C. Bake for about 40 minutes or until the pastry is golden. Leave to cool in the baking tray. Sprinkle icing sugar all over. Cut it into squares. Serve at tea time.

Note : This can be stored in an airtight container in a refrigerator for four to five days.

The Perfect Apple Pie

Serves 8

INGREDIENTS

For the Pastry

2 cups	Plain flour, sifted
1 cup	Butter (cold)
4 tbsps	Light brown sugar
2-4 tbsps	Cold water

For the Filling

7 cups	Cooking apples, thinly sliced
1 cup	Sugar
1 tsp	Cinnamon, powdered
3 tbsps	Raisins, stemmed and washed
2 tbsps	Plain flour
2 tbsps	Lemon juice
2 tbsps	Butter
A pinch of salt	

METHOD

For the Pastry

In a medium-sized mixing bowl, combine the flour and sugar. Cut the butter into small cubes and rub into the flour using fingertips until it resembles breadcrumbs. Add two tablespoons of cold water and mix well to make a smooth dough. Add more water if the dough is too dry. Form the dough into a ball, wrap it in a towel and chill for 30 minutes before using.

Divide the dough into two halves. Roll out one half in a 12 inch circle with a rolling pin. Roll from the centre outwards. Place a 9 inch pie dish on the pastry circle; the pastry should be 1inch wider all around. Carefully transfer the pastry to the pie dish. Press it gently with your fingers to fix it snugly. Refrigerate for 15 minutes. Prick it all over with a fork and bake it in an oven at 200°C or 400°F for 10-15 minutes.

For the Filling

In a small bowl, mix the sugar, flour, cinnamon and salt. In another bowl, toss apples with lemon juice. Add sugar mixture to the apples and toss it lightly to combine. Turn into the pastry-lined plate, mounding them up in the centre to support the top crust. Roll out the remaining dough into a 12 inch circle. Fold it over in quarters; cut slits for steam vents. Place the pastry in the centre and unfold to seal neatly. Crimp the edges. Bake for 45 minutes until apples are tender and the crust is golden.

Apple Crumble Pie

Serves 6-8

INGREDIENTS

For the Crust

1½ cups	*Plain flour, sieved*
¾ cup	*Cold butter*
2 tbsps	*Powdered sugar*
2 tbsps	*Cold water*
¼ tsp	*Salt*

For the Filling

6 cups	*Thinly sliced golden apples*
2 tbsps	*Lemon juice*
2 tbsps	*Plain flour*
1 tsp	*Cinnamon powder*
2-3 tbsps	*Raisins*
¼ cup	*Water*
¼ cup	*Powdered sugar*

For the Crumble

¼ cup	*Butter*
½ cup (each)	*Powdered sugar and plain flour*
¼ cup	*Rolled oats*

A pinch of salt

To Serve

Vanilla ice cream

METHOD

For the Crust: In a large bowl, combine flour, sugar and salt. Cut in butter until mixture resembles breadcrumbs. Sprinkle cold water and toss it with fork to blend lightly. When the mixture forms a ball, knead gently. Chill for 10-15 minutes. Roll into a 12 inch circle and fit it in a pie dish. Press it around gently with your fingers to fit snugly. Prick all around with a fork and refrigerate for 15 minutes. Bake in a hot oven at 150°C for 10-15 minutes. Remove and set aside.

For the Filling: Toss apples with flour, sugar, lemon juice, raisins and cinnamon powder. Arrange them on the baked pie crust. Pour water all around the apples.

For the Crumble: Mix together the oats, flour, salt and sugar. Sprinkle all over the apples. Dot with butter. Bake in a hot oven for 30 minutes or until the top is golden and crisp and apples are soft. Serve hot with vanilla ice cream.

Peach Melba Pie

Serves 8

INGREDIENTS

8" round	*Pie crust, baked*
3½ cups	*Canned, sliced peaches (reserve ¼ cup syrup)*
½ cup	*Sugar*
2 tbsps	*Corn flour*
1½ cups	*Sliced strawberries*
1 tbsp	*Butter*
500 gms	*Vanilla ice cream*
For Melba Sauce	
1 cup	*Strawberries*
2 tbsps	*Water*
1 tsp	*Corn flour*
6 tsps	*Sugar*

METHOD

For the Pie

Stir corn flour, sugar and one-fourth cup of peach syrup in a small pan and cook over medium heat until thick. Drain peaches and pour hot syrup over them. Set aside. Arrange strawberries evenly on a baked pie-crust. Cover with peach mixture and dot with butter. Cover with foil and bake at 425° F for 20-25 minutes. Remove foil for the last five minutes.

For the Sauce

Combine strawberries and one tablespoon of water in a saucepan and bring to a boil. Reduce heat and simmer until berries are soft. Dissolve corn flour in one tablespoon of water, add to the berries and cook for one minute. Remove from heat and strain. Add sugar and set aside to cool.

To Serve

Slightly cool the pie after removing from the oven. Place dollops of vanilla ice cream over the top of the pie and dribble Melba sauce over the ice cream. Serve immediately.

Note: Raspberries can be used instead of strawberries.

Glazed Peach Pie

Serves 8-10

INGREDIENTS

9" baked pie shell

For the Glaze

2½ cups	*Peaches, peeled and chopped*
1 cup	*Castor or powdered sugar*
2½ tbsps	*Corn flour*
1 tbsp	*Butter*

For the Filling

4	*Peaches, Peeled and sliced*
2 tbsps	*Peach schnappes or lemon juice*
¼ cup	*Water*
2-3 tbsps	*Sugar*
½ tsp	*Cinnamon powder*

To Serve

Vanilla ice cream or sweetened cream

METHOD

To make the glaze, crush chopped peaches and combine with sugar, corn flour and half a cup of water and bring to a boil until the mixture thickens and is translucent. Strain, add butter and cool. Gently toss peach slices with peach schnappes or lemon juice and cinnamon. Let it stand for 30 minutes and place them in a saucepan with sugar and water. Cook on a slow flame till peaches are soft but firm. Remove from stove and cool. Arrange them in the pie shell. Pour the cooled glaze over the peaches. Refrigerate for about two hours. Garnish with cream or serve with ice-cream.

Note : For pie shell refer to the pie crust recipe from perfect apple pie.

Peach Chiffon Pie

INGREDIENTS

200 gms	Marie biscuit, crushed
1 tbsp	Low-fat butter, melted
1 recipe	Low-cal whipped topping (recipe follows)
2 medium	Peaches, peeled and chopped
¾ cup	Orange juice
2 tbsps	Lemon juice
3 tsps	Gelatine powder
2 tbsps	Skim milk powder

METHOD

Combine butter, one tablespoon of orange juice and biscuit crumbs. Line one eight inch pie dish with this mixture and bake in a hot oven for five minutes. Remove and set aside to cool. Mix remaining orange juice, lemon juice and gelatine powder on a slow flame until dissolved. Let it cool slightly. Make the whipped topping. Add skimmed milk powder to gelatine mixture and whip until creamy. Fold in whipped topping to the gelatine mixture. Spread this evenly over the biscuit mixture and top it with chopped peaches. Refrigerate till firm.

Calories per serving-125; Fat content-7 g

For Whipped Topping

½ cup	Skim milk powder
⅓ cup	Cold water
¼ cup	Sugar or 4-5 sachet of sugar substitute
½ tsp	Vanilla

METHOD

Combine milk powder and water and refrigerate for 30 minutes. Beat at high speed for four minutes. Add sugar or sugar substitute little by little. Continue beating until fluffy. Add vanilla essence and refrigerate until ready to use.

Makes approx. 1 cup or 8 servings of two tablespoons each

Calories per serving-20; Fat content 6 gms

Peach and Plum Flan

Serves 6

INGREDIENTS

For the Flan Case

4 tbsps	*Butter*
3 tbsps	*Honey*
2 tbsps	*Brown sugar*
175 gms	*Muesli (semi-crushed in a food processor)*

For the Filling

2	*Fresh peaches*
4	*Fresh plums*
1	*Lemon*
6 tbsps	*Sugar*

For the Glaze

4 tbsps	*Red jelly*
2 tbsps	*Water*

To Serve

Fresh cream or vanilla ice cream

METHOD

For the Flan Case : Melt three tablespoons of the butter, honey and sugar in a saucepan over low heat. Boil gently for 30 seconds. Remove from heat and stir in the cereal. Grease a seven inch flan ring or pie tin with one tablespoon of butter and line it with the mixture. Press the mixture well to the base and sides. Bake in the centre of a moderate oven for 8-10 minutes till it is golden brown. Remove it from the oven and let it cool. When the mixture is firm, gradually ease it onto the serving plate.

For the Filling : Remove the skin from both the fruits and slice them vertically into six pieces each. You will need two small saucepans, one for each fruit. Mix three tablespoons of sugar with peach slices and cook them on a slow flame until soft, yet firm in consistency. Repeat the same with the plums.

For the Glaze : Heat water and jelly together until dissolved. Cool. Arrange peaches along the rim of the flan and the plums at the centre. Brush cooled jelly liquid over the fruit. Chill it in the fridge until ready to serve. This dish can also be served at room temperature, with sweetened whipped cream or ice-cream.

Ambrosia Cream Pie

Serves 6-8

INGREDIENTS

For the Crust

200 gms	*Ginger crunch biscuits, crushed*
2 tbsps	*Melted butter*

For the Filling

2½ cups	*Orange segments*
2 cups	*Finely chopped pineapple*
Juice of 1 lemon	
1 cup	*Milk*
2-3 tbsps	*Custard powder*
¼ cup	*Powdered sugar*
1 cup	*Whipping cream*

To Garnish

Sliced pineapple and coconut, orange segments and a few mint leaves

METHOD

For the Crust

Mix together biscuit crumbs and butter. Press this down in a eight inch pie dish and set aside.

For the Filling

Mix milk, custard powder and sugar in a saucepan and slowly heat the mixture, stirring continuously. Cook until thick. Remove from stove and cool. Whip the cream until thick. Fold into cooled custard. Mix orange, pineapple and lemon juice and add this to the custard. This whole process should be done over a bowl of ice to maintain the coolness of the mixtures. Pour this over prepared crust and chill until set. Garnish with sliced pineapple, coconut, orange and mint leaves. Serve chilled.

Piña Colada Pie

Serves 8-10

INGREDIENTS

For the Crust

20 pieces	*Ginger biscuits, crushed*
2 tbsps	*Powdered sugar*
2 tbsps	*Melted butter*
¼ cup	*Coconut, shredded*

For the Filling

1 tin (400 gms)	*Condensed milk*
100 gms	*Cream cheese*
½ cup	*Pineapple juice*
½ cup	*Thick coconut cream*
1 cup	*Fresh cream, whipped*
½ cup	*Pineapple pieces*
¼ cup	*Coconut, shredded*
2 tbsps	*Gelatine dissolved in three tablespoons of pineapple juice and strained*

To Garnish

Whipped cream, slices of pineapple and fresh coconut

METHOD

For the Crust

Mix together all the ingredients and turn put in a nine inch pie dish. Press it down with the back of a rounded spoon and bake in a warm oven for five-seven minutes or until set. Remove and set aside to cool.

For the Filling

All the ingredients should be cold. In a large bowl, mix together condensed milk, cream cheese, pineapple juice and coconut cream. Beat with an electric beater until well blended. Now fold in the whipped cream, pineapple pieces and coconut. (Reserve a few for decoration.) Lastly, add the gelatine mixture in a thin stream mixing continuously. Pour this over the crust and chill until set. Garnish with whipped cream, pineapple and coconut slices.

Strawberry Meringue Pie

Serves 6

INGREDIENTS

For the Meringue

3	*Egg whites*
170 gms	*Half castor and half icing sugar, sieved*

A pinch of cream of tartar

For the Filling

500 gms	*Strawberries*
200 gms	*Fresh cream*
1 tsp	*Lemon juice*
2 tbsps	*Icing sugar*
1 tsp	*Strawberry liqueur (optional)*

To Garnish

Sliced strawberries and grated chocolate

METHOD

For the Meringue

Grease ten inch by twelve inch rectangular baking sheet with oil. Line this with greaseproof paper. Draw an eight inch circle with pencil. Grease the paper with oil or butter. Set aside. Whisk the egg whites until stiff, add cream of tartar. Fold in the sugar gradually; beat until all the sugar is incorporated properly. Pipe or spoon the mixture onto a drawn circle on a prepared baking tray. Bake it in an oven at 110°C or 220°F or gas mark 0 for 2-3 hours, until crisp and offwhite in color. Remove from the baking sheet with a warmed palette knife. Cool and store in an airtight container.

For the Filling

Wash and clean the strawberries and crush them with a fork, reserving two-three for the top. Beat the cream in a chilled stainless steel bowl with icing sugar, strawberry liqueur (if using) and lemon juice. Keep both these chilled until use.

To Serve

Just before serving, place the meringue shell onto a serving plate. Mix strawberries with cream, spread over the shell and decorate with sliced strawberries and grated chocolate. Serve immediately.

Strawberry Margarita Pie

Serves 8-10

INGREDIENTS

For the Crust

1½ cups	*Crushed pretzel or cookies*
¼ cup	*Butter*
¼ cup	*Sugar*

For the Filling

350 gms	*Sweetened condensed milk*
1½ cups	*Chopped strawberries*
¼ cup	*Lemon juice*
¼ cup	*Tequila*
¼ cup	*Orange juice*
2 tsps	*Orange liqueur or orange essence*
1½ cups	*Whipping cream*

To Garnish

Whipping cream and strawberries slices.

METHOD

For the Crust

Mix all the ingredients in a bowl and press it down onto a nine inch pie dish. Bake it in a hot oven for five-seven minutes, remove and cool.

For the Filling

In a blender jar mix strawberries, lemon juice, tequila and orange liqueur or essence. Blend until smooth. Beat condensed milk with an electric beater and add the strawberry mixture. Whip the cream to soft peaks. Fold the cream into strawberry mixture and turn it out on a prepared crust. Cover and chill for four hours. Garnish with sliced starwberries and whipped cream.

Note: Replace Tequila with orange juice for non-alcohohic version.

Suggestion : Orange liqueur can be Triple Sec or Cointreau.

Fruit and Praline Cream Tarts

Makes 12 small tarts

INGREDIENTS

For the Tarts

200 gms	*Plain flour, sieve before measuring*
100 gms (each)	*Powdered sugar and cold butter*
A pinch of salt	
3-4 tbsps	*Cold water*

For the Filling

3 tbsps (each)	*Powdered sugar and corn flour*
1 tsp	*Vanilla essence*
¼ tsp	*Salt*
1 cup (each)	*Milk and whipping cream,*
1 cup	*Fresh fruit pieces (strawberries, oranges, kiwi)*

For the Praline

¾ cup	*Whole sugar*
½ cup	*Nuts (almonds or cashews)*

METHOD

For the Tarts

Sieve the flour and salt together in a bowl. Make a well in the centre and add the sugar and butter. Rub with fingertips, to press firmly into ball. Cover and refrigerate for an hour. Roll out the pastry one-eight inches thick to 10 inches to make a round. Cut out small rounds for tarts to fit two inch tart moulds. Bake for 10-15 minutes at 400° F. Set aside to cool.

For the Filling

Mix sugar, corn flour, salt and milk in a saucepan. Bring slowly to a boil, stirring constantly. Cook until the mixture gets thick. Remove from stove, cover and chill. When cold, stir in vanilla essence and fold in the whipped cream. Spoon this filling on the pie shell or in the tart cases. Top it with fruit pieces and sprinkle praline powder. Chill thoroughly.

For the Praline

Gently heat sugar in a heavy saucepan. Add the nuts and cook until the mixture is rich brown in colour. Remove from the stove and spread the mixture in a baking tray. Set aside to cool. Coarsely powder when the mixture is completely cold. Store in an airtight jar.

Makes 1 cup

Fresh Strawberry Glazed Pie

Serves 8-10

INGREDIENTS

9" baked pie shell

For the Glaze

2½ cups	*Medium or small strawberries, washed*
1 cup	*Castor or powdered sugar*
2½ tbsps	*Corn flour*
1 tbsp	*Butter*

For the Filling

4 cups	*Large strawberries, halved*
2 tbsps	*Cointreau or orange juice*

To Serve

Vanilla ice cream or sweetened cream

METHOD

For the Glaze

Crush the strawberries and combine with sugar and corn flour along with half a cup of water and bring to a boil until the mixture thickens and is translucent. Strain, add butter and cool.

For the Filling

Gently toss the large strawberries with the Cointreau or orange juice. Let it stand for 30 minutes.

To Assemble

Arrange in the pie shell. Pour the cool glaze over the strawberries. Refrigerate until chilled, for about two hours. Garnish with cream or serve with ice-cream.

Note : For baked pie shell refer to perfect apple pie recipe.

Fruit Pie with Cookie Crust

Serves 6-8

INGREDIENTS

For the Crust

2 cups	*Cookie crumbs*
¼ cup	*Butter*
¼ cup	*Powdered sugar*

For the Filling

½ cup	*Sugar*
3 tbsps	*Corn flour*
1 tsp	*Grated lemon rind*
1 cup	*Apple juice*
¼ cup	*Lemon juice*
3 cups	*Assorted sliced fruits*

To Garnish

Whipped cream

METHOD

For the Crust

Melt the butter in a pan; add cookie crumbs and sugar. Mix well. Press this in an eight inch pie dish and bake in a hot oven at 150°C for 5-7 minutes. Remove and set aside to cool.

For the Filling

In a heavy saucepan, mix sugar, corn flour and salt. Gradually stir in apple juice. Bring to a boil over medium heat. Cook, stirring for one minute. Remove from heat and stir in lemon juice and the rind. Cool thoroughly. Gently fold in the fruits. Turn into cookie crust. Chill for two-three hours until firm enough to cut. Garnish with whipped cream and serve cold.

Baklava

Makes 35 pieces

Baklava is a light, crisp, and delicate Middle Eastern pastry. Layers of phylo-pastry sandwiched with a pistachio and walnut mixture and sugar syrup makes it a all-time favorite dish.

INGREDIENTS

For the Pastry

500 gms	*Phylo or puff pastry (readymade)*
100 gms	*Shortening or unsalted butter*
300 gms	*Finely-ground pistachio, walnuts or almonds (or a mixture of all three)*
1/4 cup	*Powdered sugar*

For the Syrup

1 cup	*Sugar*
1/4 cup	*Honey*
3/4 cup	*Water*
1 tbsp	*Lemon juice*

A few saffron threads

To Garnish

Rose petals

METHOD

Open out the puff pastry on a floured board. You will need a large deep baking tray, preferably a Swiss roll pan. Grease the tray with butter or shortening. Roll out the dough very lightly, using a little flour, if required, to match the size of your tray. Place this on the tray and brush it with shortening or butter. Mix one-two tablespoons of water with nuts and spread them over the pastry. Cover with the remaining pastry, brushing with shortening or butter. You could make three layers of this if you wish, brushing each one with shortening or butter. Finally, seal the pastry from the sides by pressing the top layer down to the bottom one. If you are using phylo pastry, brush each layer with shortening or butter and use five-six layers before putting the nuts and 5-6 layers on top. Mark diagonally with a sharp knife diamond or square-shaped pieces, dipping the knife in hot water for easier cutting. Bake the baklava for 45 minute in a preheated oven at 325°F, then raise the heat to 400°F and bake for 10 more minutes. The baklava should be golden in colour.

While it is baking, prepare the syrup by mixing sugar, honey and water until thick enough to coat a spoon. Allow it to cool completely. Add lemon juice and saffron.

Remove baklava from the oven and quickly pour the cold syrup over the hot baklava. Sprinkle chopped nuts all over and leave it to cool slightly. Cut into pieces of pastry and place them on a serving dish, sprinkled with some more nuts if you wish. Garnish with rose petals around. These taste superb served hot!

Note : When you pour syrup over baklava, it is either cold syrup on hot baklava or hot syrup over cold baklava. You must never pour hot syrup over hot baklava. This can make the pastry soggy.

Chocolate Crunch Pie

Serves 6

INGREDIENTS

For the Crust

200 gms	*Digestive biscuits, powdered*
½ cup	*Brown sugar*
2 tbsps	*Melted butter*

For the Filling

150 gms	*Semi-sweet chocolate, broken into pieces*
¼ cup	*Milk*
1 tsp	*Vanilla essence*
200 gms	*Fresh cream*
3 tbsps	*Icing sugar*

To Garnish

Grated chocolate and whipped cream

METHOD

For the Crust

Melt butter in a saucepan, add biscuit crumbs and sugar. Mix well. Take it off the stove and set aside to cool. Spread this mixture into a eight inch pie dish and press it to give a neat look. Set aside.

For the Filling

In a medium saucepan, heat chocolate and milk until melted. Remove from stove and cool. Beat the cream with icing sugar and vanilla. Gently fold it in the chocolate mixture and pour this over the biscuit crust. Put this in the freezer compartment until set. Remove and garnish with grated chocolate and cream. Serve chilled.

Baklava

Chocolate Crunch Pie

Gâteau Mount Blanc

Gâteau Mount Blanc

Serves 8-10

INGREDIENTS

For the Choux Pastry

7½ fl oz or 200 ml	*Water*
2½ oz or 65 gms	*Butter*
3¾ oz or 100 gms	*Plain flour, well sieved*
3	*Eggs, beaten*

A pinch of salt, a pinch of sugar and one tablespoon of vanilla, if sweet

For the Cream Filling

300 gms	*Fresh cream*
½ tsp	*Vanilla essence*
5 tbsps	*Powdered sugar*
1½ tbsps	*Kirsch (optional)*

For the Chocolate Sauce

200 gms	*Semi-sweet cooking chocolate*
¾ cup	*Milk and cream, mixed*
50 gms	*Butter*
2 tbsps	*Icing sugar*
¼ cup	*Additional cream, if required*
1 tsp	*Vanilla essence*

METHOD

For the Choux Pastry

Pre heat the oven to 180°C. In a heavy saucepan, boil the water, add salt and butter. As soon as the liquid rises, like milk, remove from heat and add sugar and vanilla. Add the flour all at once and beat vigorously with a wooden spoon to obtain a smooth paste. Replace on low heat, till the mixture dries out. Make sure it does not stick to the pan. Remove from heat and allow it to cool. Using a rotary beater, beat in the egg liquid, little by little, until all the egg has been absorbed thoroughly. Ensure that the mixture does not become runny. Butter the baking sheet lightly. Fill the icing bag with the pastry and pipe the profiteroles in a diameter of two centimetre, keeping a little space between them to rise. Bake for 20-25 minutes. Do not open the oven in the first 15 minutes or else the choux will collapse. Remove from the oven once they are firm and golden. Leave to cool on a wire rack.

Makes 30 profiteroles

For the Cream Filling

In order to whip the cream successfully, it must be whisked in a very cold stainless steel bowl in a cool place. Pour the cold cream in the bowl. Whip it with a whisk, if necessary place the bowl over ice cubes. When the cream starts to thicken, add sugar, one spoon at a time. Add vanilla and kirsch (it using). If not using immediately, refrigerate until use.

For the Chocolate Sauce : Break the chocolate into pieces, melt gently in a double boiler. When melted, transfer it into a heavy saucepan and add the cream-milk mixture, butter and vanilla. Allow to cool. Add sugar and mix well. Add additional whipped cream if the sauce is too liquid.

Makes 1½ cups of Chocolate Sauce

Assembling The Gâteau : Slit each profiterole with a knife. Fill it with the whipped cream with a piping bag. Pile up the profiteroles like a mountain on a deep serving plate, pain the warm chocolate sauce over and finally pipe the tip of the pile with cream. Chill for several hours. Serve with the remaining chocolate sauce at the side.

Tip : Sprinkle little water around the piped choux pastry. This creates the steam while baking, which will help the pastry to rise more. As a result you will have a lighter product.

Fruit Cereal Pie

Serves 6-8

INGREDIENTS

For the Crust

2 cups	*Crushed wheat cereal*
2 tbsps	*Fruit juice*
¼ cup	*Chopped nuts and raisins*

For the Filling

1 cup	*Low fat Yogurt*
1 cup	*Low fat whipping cream*
2-3 tsps	*Sugar or 1 sachet sugar substitute*
2 cups	*Sliced fruit*
1 tbsp	*Lemon juice*

A pinch of cinnamon powder

METHOD

For the Crust: Mix all the ingredients in a bowl and press in a pie dish. Set aside.

For the Filling: Sieve the yogurt to get a smooth creamy texture. Whip the cream to form soft peaks. Add lemon juice and sugar. Spread this over pie-crust. Toss fruit with cinnamon powder and arrange over the yogurt mixture. Chill until ready to serve.

Plum Galette

Serves 8

INGREDIENTS

For the Dough

2 cups	*Plain flour*
1 tbsp	*Powdered sugar*
1 tbsp	*Maize flour*
½ tsp	*Baking powder*
½ tsp	*Salt*
1 cup	*Butter, chilled and cut into pieces*
2 tbsps	*Cream*
2 tbsps	*Chilled water*

For the Filling

2½ cups	*Purple plums, pitted and sliced*
½ cup	*Powdered sugar (reserve two tablespoons for sprinkling)*
3 tbsps	*Plain flour*
3 tbsps	*Ground almonds*
¼ tsp	*Cinnamon powder*
1 tbsp	*Butter*
1 medium	*Egg, beaten with little water OR milk to brush*

METHOD

For the Dough

Sieve the flour, sugar, maize flour, baking powder and salt in a bowl. Cut in the butter using your fingertips to resemble a coarse meal. Combine cream and water and blend in until the dough comes together. Shape into a round ball, cover and chill for 15 minutes. Roll out the dough on a lightly floured board into a 14" round circle, about one-eight inch thick. Transfer it to a baking sheet lined with greaseproof paper.

For the Filling

In a small bowl, combine one-fourth cup of sugar with ground almonds, flour and cinnamon. Spread this evenly over the dough to within two inches of the edge. Arrange the plum wedges on top and dot with butter. Set aside two tablespoons from remaining sugar and sprinkle the rest over plums. Fold the edges of the dough up over the plums to create a two inch border. Bake the galette at 375°F for about 35 to 40 minutes or until crust is golden brown. If any juices have leaked onto the baking sheet, slide knife under the galette to release it from the sheet. Sprinkle sugar and cool to room temperature before serving.

Almond/Hazelnut Galettes with Caramelised Apples

Serves 4

INGREDIENTS

For the Pastry

175 gms	Softened butter
4 tbsps	Powdered sugar
225 gms	Plain flour
175 gms	Ground almonds or hazelnuts

For Caramelised Apples

100 gms	Butter
100 gms	Powdered brown sugar
6 large	Dessert apples, peeled cored and sliced

To Serve

150 ml	Whipping cream
3 tbsps	Icing sugar

METHOD

Beat the butter and sugar until light and fluffy. Fold in the flour and ground almonds. Divide the mixture into two balls, place in plastic bags and chill well in the fridge for 10 minutes. Preheat the oven at 180°C 350°F. Line a baking tray with greaseproof paper. Roll out the pastry on a floured surface to one-fourth inch thickness. Cut it into 12 three inch circles. Transfer to the prepared baking tray and bake in preheated oven for 10 minutes. Cool.

For Caramelised Apples

Melt the butter; add the sugar and then apples. Using a wooden spoon, turn the mixture time to time. Cook gently till apples are brown and toffee-like. Set aside to cool.

Whip the cream with half the icing sugar until soft peaks form and fill it in piping bag.

To Assemble

Take two of the biscuits and sandwich them with cooled caramelised apple mixture. Spread some more apple mixture on the top biscuit and crown with the third biscuit. Pipe whipped cream round the edge of the biscuit layers. Dust the top with icing sugar. Repeat for the remaining biscuits. Serve cold.

Blueberry Delight

Serves 8

INGREDIENTS

For the Crust

1 cup	Plain flour, sieved
3/4 cup	Powdered almonds
1/2 cup	Butter, softened
1/4 cup	Powdered brown sugar

For the Filling

200 gms	Cream cheese, softened
3/4 cup	Powdered sugar
1 cup	Whipping cream (whipped)
1 tsp	Vanilla essence

For the Topping

1/2 cup	Dried blueberries, soaked in little water or 250 gms fresh blueberries.
1 tbsp	Corn flour
1 tbsp	Sugar
1/4 cup	Blueberry preserve
1 tsp	Butter

Juice of 1 lemon

METHOD

Cream butter in a bowl and mix in all the ingredients for the pastry and press it into a 13 inch x 9 inch pan. Bake for 15 minutes at 150°C. Remove and set aside to cool.

For the Filling

Beat cream cheese in a bowl with an electric beater. Gradually add sugar and vanilla. Fold in the beaten cream and spread this onto a cooled pie-crust.

For the Topping

Mix all the ingredients in a saucepan and bring to a boil. Heat until thickened. Cool and spread over filling. Chill until ready to serve. Cut into two inch square pieces to serve.

Note : Fresh blueberries will require longer boiling time compared to the dried ones.

Mango Delight

Serves 6

INGREDIENTS

For the Crust

16-18	*Oatmeal, ginger or digestive biscuits, crushed*
2 tbsps	*Butter*
2 tbsps	*Powdered sugar*

For the Filling

1 cup (each)	*Mango pulp, cream cheese and whipping cream*
1 piece	*Alphonso mango, peeled and sliced*
1 tsp	*Lemon juice*

Sugar as required

To Garnish

Mint leaves, crystallized ginger

METHOD

For the Crust

Melt butter in a saucepan, add the biscuit crumbs and sugar. Mix well.

Line a eight inch pie dish with this mixture and press down firmly. Bake in hot oven for 5-6 minutes and cool.

For the Filling

Beat cream cheese and chilled mango pulp together until smooth. Whip the cream until it forms soft peaks. Fold in the cream into the mango-cheese mixture. Add the lemon juice and mix well. Pour this over the cooled crust and set in the refrigerator for two hours. Garnish before serving.

Note: For a firmer pie, cook two teaspoons of gelatine in three tablespoons of water till transparent and fold it in the mixture at the end and then pour over the crust.

Orange Delight

Serves 6

INGREDIENTS

18	*Light digestive biscuits*
2 tbsps	*Concentrated orange juice*
1 tsp	*Lemon juice*
3 cups	*Orange segments*
1 cup	*Fat-free cream cheese or thick yogurt made with skimmed milk*
½ cup	*Orange slices*
4 tsps	*Gelatine dissolved in five tablespoons of orange juice*
Low fat butter	
Sugar substitute	

To Garnish

Sliced oranges

METHOD

Crush the digestive biscuits. Spray a pie dish with low fat spray. Combine crushed biscuits, orange juice concentrate and lemon juice in a bowl and mix well. Line the dish with this mixture and chill till it sets. In the meanwhile, combine orange segments, sugar and cream cheese or yogurt. Warm the gelatine mixture slightly and add to the orange mixture in a thin stream stirring continuously. Pour this mixture over the biscuit crust and chill again. Garnish with sliced oranges before serving.

Note: As a variation you can use strawberries in place of oranges.

175 calories per serving, three gms fat.

Lemon Cream Pie

Serves 8-10

INGREDIENTS

For the Pastry

200 gms	*Plain flour*
100 gms	*Cold butter*
1 tsp	*Powdered sugar*

For the Filling

1 large packet	*Lemon jelly*
1 tsp	*Lemon rind, grated*
3 tbsps	*Powdered sugar*
½ tsp	*Lemon essence*
300 gms	*Fresh cream*

Juice of 2 lemons

To Garnish

Whipped cream and lemon slices

METHOD

For the Pastry

Sieve the flour and sugar together. Cut the butter into pieces and rub into the flour using fingertips. The mixture should resemble breadcrumbs. Add just enough two-three tablespoons of cold water to bind the dough. Cover and place the dough in the fridge for half an hour. Lightly flour a rolling pin and the rolling surface that you want to roll the pastry on. Roll the pastry to fit a eight inch pie dish. Prick it with a fork all around and bake in a hot oven 400°F for 10-12 minutes. Cool the pastry shell.

For the Filling

Dissolve the jelly in one cup of boiling water. Cool it a little and add half a cup of cold water, lemon juice and lemon rind. Set partially in the freezer compartment. Remove and break it up with a beater. Beat the cream in a stainless steel bowl with sugar and lemon essence. Mix one and a half cups of cream with the jelly mixture, reserving the rest for the decoration. Mix the jelly and cream mixture well and pour it into the baked pie dish. Put in the freezer until set. Remove and decorate with the remaining cream and lemon slices.

Lemon Mousse Pie

Serves 8

INGREDIENTS

9" round	*Baked pie shell*
2 tbsps	*Gelatine powder*
½ cup	*Lemon juice*
¼ cup	*Water*
200 gms	*Philadelphia cream cheese*
1 cup	*Icing sugar*
1 cup	*Whipped cream*
1 tsp	*Grated lemon rind*

To Garnish

¼ cup	*Lemon jelly powder mixed with ¼ cup of hot water*

A few mint leaves and lemon slices

METHOD

Combine gelatine, lemon juice and water. Stir until dissolved and transparent. Pass it through the sieve. Add the rind and set aside to cool. In a large bowl, combine cream cheese and sugar. Beat until smooth. Blend gelatine mixture slowly and continue beating over ice. Fold in the whipped cream and pour over pie shell. Chill for one hour. Meanwhile cool the lemon jelly over ice until it just begins to set. Quickly spread over the pie and chill. Just before serving, garnish with mint leaves and lemon slices.

Mango Cottage Cheese Pie

Serves 8

INGREDIENTS

For the Base

200 gms packet	*Flavoured Marie biscuits, toasted and crumbed*
4 tbsps	*Melted butter*
2 tbsps	*Powdered sugar*

For the Filling

2	*Ripe Alphonso mangoes, peeled and sliced*
400 gms	*Crumbled cottage cheese (chhenna)*
1/4 cup	*Thick cream*
1/4 cup	*Powdered sugar*
1/4 cup	*Mango pulp*
2-3 drops	*Rose water (optional)*

To Garnish

Whipped cream and slivered and toasted pistachios

METHOD

For the base

Mix all the ingredients for the base and press down in the pie dish. Chill.

For the filling

In a medium bowl, beat together crumbled cottage cheese, cream, sugar and mango pulp until smooth. Add rose water (if using). Spread this mixture over the prepared base and chill for half an hour or more. Arrange mango slices in a wheel pattern over the cottage cheese mixture. Garnish with cream and pistachios. Refrigerate until ready to serve.

Pecan Pie

Serves 8

INGREDIENTS

1 8" round	*Baked pie shell*
½ cup	*Brown sugar*
½ cup	*Butter*
½ cup	*Water, mixed with two tablespoons of corn flour*
¾ cup	*Whole sugar*
1 cup	*Thick cream*
1 cup	*Toasted halved pecan nuts*
¼ cup	*Chopped pecan nuts*
½ tsp	*Vanilla essence*
A pinch of salt	

METHOD

In a double boiler top, beat brown sugar, butter until blended. Add whole sugar, salt, corn flour mixture and cream. Mix well. Cook over boiling water, stirring from time to time. Remove from water and stir in the halved pecan nuts and vanilla. Pour this mixture over a baked pie shell and spread evenly. Bake for 30 minutes. Remove and sprinkle chopped nuts on top and bake again for five more minutes. Remove from the oven and set aside to cool. Serve at room temperature.

Brownie Banana Split Pizza

Serves 8-10

INGREDIENTS

For the Brownie

¼ cup (each)	*Powdered sugar and brown sugar*
1 cup (each)	*Plain flour, sieved and ice cold water*
1 tsp (each)	*Baking powder and vanilla essence*
½ tsp	*Soda bi carb*
¼ tsp	*Salt*
3 tbsps	*Cocoa powder*
6 tbsps	*Melted butter*
⅓ cup	*Chopped walnuts*
1 tbsp	*Vinegar*

For the Topping

½ cup (each)	*Cream cheese and condensed milk*
¼ cup	*Orange juice*
3-4 pieces	*Small sized bananas*
2 tbsps	*Lemon juice*
1 cup	*Sliced strawberries*
1 tsp	*Vanilla essence*
¼ cup (each)	*Chopped nuts and chopped cooking chocolate*
1 tbsp	*Butter*

METHOD

For the Brownies

Sieve together plain flour, baking powder, soda, salt, powdered sugar and cocoa. Place this in a mixing bowl and add the remaining ingredients. Mix well. Grease 12" pie dish and pour this mixture evenly. Bake in a hot oven at 350°F for 20 minutes. Remove and cool in the pan for 5-7 minutes and then on the rack.

For the Topping

In a small bowl, mix cream cheese condensed milk, vanilla and orange juice until light. Set aside to chill. Slice the bananas diagonally and dribble lemon juice over them. Transfer the brownie base onto a serving plate and spoon cream cheese mixture over and spread evenly. Arrange banana slices on cream cheese mixture. Add sliced strawberries and chopped nuts on top. In a small saucepan melt chocolate and butter. Drizzle over the fruits. Chill. Cut into wedges and serve.

Fruits, Ice-creams and Sorbets

If desserts, nostalgic with old-fashioned goodness are your weakness or, if a show-stopping sensation is your aim or the heat of the afternoon sun has bothered you, this is a perfect choice to soothe your nerves. Sorbets are perfect to whet your appetite between meals and freshen your palate.

Double Chocolate Chip Ice-cream

Serves 6-8

INGREDIENTS

½ cup	*Plain chocolate, broken into pieces + two tablespoons of cocoa*
1 cup	*Milk*
3	*Egg yolks*
⅓ cup	*Sugar*
1 ½ cups	*Fresh cream*
¼ cup	*Chocolate, chopped*

METHOD

Stir the chocolate pieces and cocoa with milk in a saucepan over low heat, until the chocolate melts and the mixture is smooth. Whisk the egg yolks with the sugar in a mixing bowl, until the mixture falls off the whisk in a thick ribbon. Gradually add the chocolate-flavoured milk, whisking constantly. Pour the mixture back into the saucepan and stir over medium heat, until it thickens and coats the back of the spoon. Strain into a bowl and cool in the refrigerator. When cold, fold in the whipped cream. Pour the mixture into a churner, add the chopped chocolate and churn until set.

Note : For the eggless variation, replace egg yolks with six tablespoons of condensed milk and reduce sugar to one-fourth cup.

Coffee Ice-cream

Makes approx. 1 kg

INGREDIENTS

1½ cups	*Full fat milk*
1	*Egg yolks*
6-8 tbsps	*Sugar*
1½ cups	*Thick cream*
4 tbsps	*Espresso coffee OR*
4 tsps	*Instant coffee, mixed with one-fourth cup of water*
1 tsp	*Camp coffee or vanilla essence*

METHOD

Heat the milk. Beat egg yolks and sugar in a bowl until light. Continue beating and add hot milk. Transfer this mixture to a heavy saucepan and cook over a medium heat, stirring constantly. Cook until the custard is thick and coats the back of the spoon. Do not allow the mixture to boil or it will curdle. Stir in the cream, coffee and the essence. Remove from stove and strain the mixture through a sieve. Allow it to cool to room temperature. Pour the mixture in an ice-cream machine and churn as per manufacture's instructions. Alternately, freeze the mixture in seven cup capacity metal box over night or until it sets.

Double Chocolate Chip Ice-cream

Coffee Ice-cream

Fruit Salsa with Cinnamon Chips

Lychee Kulfi

Lychee Kulfi
(Lychee flavoured Indian Ice-cream)

Makes 6-8 pieces

INGREDIENTS

1½ litres	*Milk*
⅓ cup	*Sugar*
½ tin (200 gms)	*Condensed milk*
1 cup	*Lychee pulp, sieved (approx. 16-18 pieces)*

METHOD

Heat the milk in a heavy saucepan until a one-fourth part is reduced. Add sugar and boil again till it is reduced to half. Remove from stove and set aside to cool. Add condensed milk and lychee pulp. Mix well. Fill the kulfi moulds with this mixture and freeze overnight. To remove kulfi from the moulds, rub the mould with both your palms and slightly loosen the kulfi and serve in a small ice cream cone or a bowl.

Variation

Replace lychees with fruit pulp of your choice such as custard apple, mango, mixed dry fruits, strawberries, etc.

To use ready kulfi mix, reduce milk to half litre, omit sugar and reduce condensed milk to one-fourth cup. Make as directed on the box, cool and then add the fruit pulp.

Note : You can also set kulfi in small earthern pots.

Fruit Salsa With Cinnamon Chips

Serves 6-8

INGREDIENTS

2 (each)	*Kiwi and golden apples, peeled and diced*
2 cups	*Segmented orange, chopped peaches, pears, strawberries*
2 tbsps (each)	*Powdered sugar and lemon juice*
3 tbsps	*Orange marmalade*
6 (10")	*Tortillas*
1 cup	*Castor sugar mixed with one tsp of cinnamon powder*

Butter to brush the tortillas

METHOD

In a stainless steel bowl, mix together sugar, lemon juice and marmalade. Add all the fruit. Mix well. Refrigerate for one-two hours. Brush tortillas with a little butter, cut into wedges, arrange in a single layer on a baking sheet. Sprinkle with desired amount of sugar and bake in a hot oven for eight-ten minutes or until crisp. Allow to cool for 10-15 minutes. Serve with chilled salsa.

Fruit Compote

Serves 8

INGREDIENTS

½ cup	*Prunes*
½ cup	*Apricots*
½ cup	*Pitted cherries*
½ cup	*Figs*
½ cup	*Port wine*
1¾ cups	*Water*
1 cup	*Orange juice*
2 tbsps	*Sugar*
1" stick	*Cinnamon*

METHOD

Combine all the ingredients in a saucepan and bring to boil. Reduce heat and simmer for thirty minutes. Discard cinnamon stick and cool the compote. Fill in a jar and store in the refrigerator until needed. Serve with vanilla ice cream, hot or cold.

Ice-cream Crunch

Serves 6

INGREDIENTS

350 gms	*Ginger biscuits, finely crushed*
⅓ cup	*Butter*
150 gms	*Chopped chocolate*
1 litre	*Vanilla ice cream*
1 cup	*Sliced fruit of your choice (banana, pineapple, etc.)*
3 tsps	*Maple syrup*

Juice of ½ a lemon

To Garnish

Slivered and toasted almonds

METHOD

Melt butter and chocolate over low heat. Remove and add crushed biscuit crumbs; press the mixture into a shallow pie dish. Refrigerate for about one hour. Prepare the fruit and soak in lemon juice. Just before serving, arrange half the fruit on the base of the prepared pie dished. Fill with scoops of ice-cream, arrange remaining fruits over them and pour maple syrup. Garnish with almonds and serve at once.

Chocolate Avalanche

Serves 8

INGREDIENTS

8 pieces	*Chocolate brownies (recipe on page 250)*
500 gms	*Malted chocolate ice cream*
1 cup	*Chocolate fudge sauce*
1 cup	*Whipping cream*
½ cup	*Toasted and chopped hazelnuts*
5-6 pieces	*Sponge fingers or cake cubes*

To Garnish

Additional whipped cream, chocolate rice and chocolate wafer sticks

METHOD

Arrange the brownies in individual bowls or in a deep transparent glass bowl. Scoop chocolate ice-cream on top of the brownie pieces and dribble fudge sauce over. Pipe whipped cream in between the layers. Dip sponge fingers in the sauce and stick them around the ice cream. Sprinkle nuts all over. Garnish with whipped cream, chocolate rice and chocolate sticks. Serve immediately.

Chocolate fudge sauce

In a heavy saucepan, mix together 100 gms of cooking chocolate, one-fourth cup each of milk and cream, two tablespoons of powdered sugar, half a tablespoon of vanilla essence, one tablespoon of butter and a small pinch of salt. Boil until thick. Cool.

Makes ¾ cup

Tiramisu Ice-cream

Serves 8

INGREDIENTS

6-8 pieces	*Sponge fingers, broken into pieces*
2 tbsps	*Kahlua or strong coffee*
500 gms	*Coffee ice cream*
2 tbsps	*Instant coffee dissolved in two tablespoons of water*
200 gms (each)	*Mascarpone cheese and beaten fresh cream*
½ cup	*Powdered sugar*
2 tsp	*Camp coffee or vanilla essence*
100 gms	*Fine quality chocolate, chopped*

METHOD

Chill serving bowl or mould thoroughly. In a small bowl, soak sponge fingers with Kahlua or coffee. Combine Mascarpone and sugar in a bowl and beat for two minutes. Fold in the beaten cream and the essence. Set aside. Slightly soften the ice-cream and add strong coffee. Mix well. Take a serving bowl and layer half of the Mascarpone mixture at the bottom, top it with coffee ice-cream and chopped chocolate and gently swirl in the soaked sponge fingers. Repeat with all the layers. Smoothen the top. Cover the bowl tightly with cling wrap or foil and freeze over-night. Serve chilled from the serving bowl or unmould on a deep plate.

Passionfruit Sherbet

Serves 6

INGREDIENTS

12 large	*Passionfruits*
1 cup	*Sugar*
3 cups	*Water*
¼ cup	*Lemon juice*

METHOD

Cut fruit into half and scoop out pulp. Strain and remove seeds. The pulp should measure ¾ cup. Place sugar in a pan with one cup of water and bring to a boil. Remove from stove and cool completely. Add passionfruit pulp, lemon juice and remaining water. Pour into a lamington tin and freeze until set. Blend in a mixer until smooth. Return to pan and freeze until set. Scoop with an ice-cream spoon and serve with fresh fruits.

Mint Chocolate Chips Cheesecake Ice-Cream

Serves 4-6

INGREDIENTS

½ cup	Cream cheese
½ cup	Chocolate chips
¼ cup	Condensed milk
¼ cup	Shipping cream
1 tsp	Gelatine mixed with two tablespoons of water
1 tsp	Mint or vanilla essence
500 gms	Vanilla ice cream, softened
5-6 pieces	After Eight Chocolate Mint Thins

METHOD

In a medium bowl, beat cream cheese with condensed milk until light. Whip the cream in a separate bowl until stiff. Fold it into the cheese mixture. Cook gelatine with water on a slow flame till melted. Cool. Add mint essence and pour this liquid in a thin stream in to the cheese mixture while beating. Do this over a bowl of ice cubes. When the mixture begins to set, remove from ice and set aside. Gently fold in the chocolate chips into the cheese mixture. Fold in softened ice cream and freeze for half an hour until firm. Remove and layer half of the ice-cream mixture in an aluminum tin. Layer pieces of After Eight chocolate pieces (set aside two for garnish). Top it with remaining ice-cream and freeze for four-five hours or overnight. To serve, unmould the ice cream with and decorate with the remaining chocolates.

Honey Nut Ice-cream

Serves 10-12

INGREDIENTS

1½ litres	*Milk*
2 tbsps	*Corn flour*
1 ½ cups	*Sugar*
1 tsp	*Gelatine, melted with 3 tbsp of water*
200 gms	*Fresh cream*
¼ cup (each)	*Walnut and cashews, finely chopped*
½ cup	*Fig, cut into pieces*
¼ cup	*Honey*
¼ cup	*Water*

METHOD

Boil the milk for 30 minutes. Dissolve corn flour in a little cold milk and add to the boiling milk along with sugar. Stir constantly until thick. Remove from the gas and cool. Add the melted gelatine and fresh cream. Combine the walnuts, cashews, figs, honey and water in a small saucepan and heat on the gas. Then cool. Add to the prepared milk. Cover the pan and chill for 15-20 minutes. Make ice-cream in a churner. Transfer it to a metal box and store in the freezer.

Tropical Fruit Salad with Mango-Walnut Cream

Serves 6

INGREDIENTS

4-5 cups	*Mixed fruit, (pineapple, apple, melon, orange, strawberries, kiwi, banana, etc.)*
Juice of ½ a lemon	
1 cup (each)	*Whipped cream and thick mango pulp*
½ cup	*Finely chopped toasted walnuts*

METHOD

Cut the pineapple, apple, melon and banana in cubes, peel the oranges and slice the strawberries and kiwis. Mix all the fruits in a bowl. Dribble lemon juice over, cover and chill. Whip the cream until soft peaks form. Fold in the mango pulp and toasted walnuts. Cover and chill for one-two hours. Serve fruit salad with chilled cream.

Fluffy Fruit Dip

Makes 2 cups

INGREDIENTS

1½ cups	*Whipping cream*
2 tbsps	*Lemon juice*
4 tbsps	*Sugar*
¼ tsp	*Powdered cinnamon*
1 tbsp (each)	*Lemon and orange zest*
3 tbsps	*Peach schappes (optional) ground almonds and Peach schnapps (optional)*

To Serve

Sweet biscuits, sponge cake pieces or fruit pieces

METHOD

Place cream in a stainless steel bowl and whip over a bowl of ice, with sugar and lemon juice until stiff peaks form. Fold in cinnamon, lemon and orange zest, almond and Peach schnapps (if using). Cover and chill. Serve with biscuits, cake pieces or fruits.

Orange Sorbet

Serves 8-10

INGREDIENTS

3½ cups	*Fresh orange juice, strained (8-10 oranges)*
200 gms	*Sugar*
Juice of 3 lemons	

METHOD

When you extract the orange juice, put the pulp of 2-3 oranges through a blender and add this to the juice. Add sugar, stirring with a wooden spoon until the sugar dissolves completely. Add the juice and mix. Pour into a copper bottom stainless steel pan and freeze. You must prevent crystallization during freezing. Freeze the mixture for one hour, remove and cut lumps. Put these through the food processor until completely smooth. Repeat two-three times. When the sorbet is nearly frozen, take it out, beat well and put it back into the freezer or the mould you wish to use. Freeze for 30 minutes, so the sorbet will not turn into hard ice cubes. Scoop it out with an ice-cream serving spoon and serve in stemmed glasses.

Fluffy Fruit Dip

Island Fruit Compote

Nougat Basket

Island Fruit Compote

Serves 4-6

INGREDIENTS

2 cups	*Mixed fresh fruit, peeled and chopped (red and green grapes, kiwi, orange, pineapple)*
250 gms	*Sugar*
1 cup	*Water*
2 tsps	*Lemon juice*
1" stick	*Cinnamon*
1 large	*Papaya*
2-3 tsps	*Brandy (optional)*
1 cups	*Whipping cream*

To Garnish : *2 tbsps of slivered almonds and 6-8 glace cherries*

To Serve: *Vanilla ice cream*

METHOD

Mix sugar, cinnamon and water in a saucepan and bring to a boil. Continue cooking until sugar has melted. Remove from stove and add lemon juice. Soak chopped fruits in this syrup. Cut the papaya into half and remove seeds. Spoon the fruit into each half of the papaya. Chill. Beat the cream to stiff peaks and fill it in a piping bag. Pipe on over the fruit, making sure to seal the exposed fruit surface. Do not cover the base of the papaya. Sprinkle with slivered almonds and cherries. Serve with vanilla ice-cream.

Peach Ice-cream

Serves 8

INGREDIENTS

1½ kg	*Fresh peaches, washed peeled and chopped*
½ cup	*Powdered sugar*
2 cups	*Thick cream*
400 gms (1 can)	*Sweetened condensed milk*
2½ cups	*Full fat milk*
1 tsp	*Vanilla essence*

A pinch of cinnamon powder

METHOD

Puree peaches with sugar and cream in a blender. Remove and mix together condensed milk, milk, vanilla essence and cinnamon powder. Pour this in an ice-cream container and churn until set or put it in a metal box in the freezer compartment until set.

Nougat Basket

Serves 12-15

INGREDIENTS

½ cup	*Cashew nuts*	*coarsely powdered*
½ cup	*Peanuts, without the skin*	
1 ½ cup	*Sugar*	
2 tsps	*Sugar, for the handle*	

A little oil

Vanilla or butterscotch ice-cream for serving

METHOD

Place the sugar in a very thick vessel, heat and slowly let it melt, stirring from time to time. Add the nuts, mix well and take the mixture off the flame immediately. Oil the working surface, two knives and a bowl. Pour the mixture on the working surface and work it with the two knives until it forms a dough. Take three-fourths of it and roll it thinly as quickly as possible. Press this rolled dough in the oiled bowl to form a basket in the shape of the bowl. Let it cool and remove it very gently. Then place it over a serving plate or keep it in an airtight container. To make the handle of the basket, roll out the remaining dough. If it has hardened, re-heat it slightly. Roll it out into a long strip and bend into a "U" shape while hot. Melt two tablespoons of sugar in a small vessel, dip the ends of the strip in it and stick it firmly to the bowl to form a handle. Fill your nougat basket with ice-cream or fresh fruit and serve.

Lemon and Pineapple Ice-Cream

Serves 8

INGREDIENTS

1 tin (450 gms)	*Pineapple slices*
¾ cup	*Sugar*
1 tbsp	*Gelatine*
3 tbsps	*Lemon juice*
½ litre	*Milk, boiled and cooled*
2 cups	*Fresh cream, beaten*

METHOD

Liquidize pineapple slices with the syrup. Mix sugar and gelatine powder along with pineapple pulp. Heat the mixture till gelatine and sugar dissolve. Remove from fire and cool. Add lemon juice and milk. Place this mixture over a bowl of ice cubes and beat with an egg-beater. When the mixture begins to set, add the cream and continue beating till all the cream is incorporated. Either freeze it in a metal box or churn it in an ice-cream machine.

Lychee Ice-cream

Serves 6

INGREDIENTS

2 cups	*Lychee pulp (approx. 30 lychees)*
½ cup	*Chopped lychees*
1 cup	*Sugar*
1 tbsp	*Gelatine*
200 gms	*Fresh cream*
2 cups	*Milk, boiled for 20 minutes and cooled*
½ tsp	*Lemon juice*

METHOD

Mix together lychee pulp, lemon juice and sugar. Mix gelatine in little water and add to the lychee pulp. Heat this mixture on a slow fire and cook until sugar melts and the gelatine is dissolved. Remove from fire and set aside to cool. Add chopped lychees, cream and milk. Mix well till all the ingredients are properly combined. Pour this in a metal container, cover and freeze or pass it through an ice-cream machine till it sets.

Strawberries and Oranges with Honey Yogurt Topping

Serves 8

INGREDIENTS

500 gms	*Fresh strawberries, washed and sliced*
3 large	*Oranges, peeled*
2-3 tbsps	*Grand Marnier*
Honey Yogurt Topping	
1 cup	*Whipping cream*
¾ cup	*Thick yogurt*
2-3 tbsps	*Honey*

To Serve

Top the fruit with honey yogurt topping and serve

METHOD

Mix strawberries, oranges and Grand Marnier in a bowl. Cover and refrigerate for several hours.

For Honey Yogurt Topping : Whip the cream until it begins to thicken. Beat in honey, beat until thick. Fold in the yogurt. Refrigerate for several hours.

Watermelon Ice

Serves 10

INGREDIENTS

½ small	*Watermelon, cut into cubes (700 gms)*
3 level tbsps	*Icing sugar*
1 tbsp	*Lemon juice*
¼ level tsp	*Salt*

METHOD

Put one cup of watermelon pieces in a blender jar along with icing sugar, lemon juice and salt. Blend until smooth. Add the remaining fruit and blend again. Pour this mixture in a shallow freezer tray and freeze for two hours. Spoon the mixture into a chilled bowl and beat it with electric beater until fluffy. Return it to a freezer container, cover and freeze again until firm. Leave at room temperature for five-seven minutes before serving. Scoop into individual bowls and serve.

Custards, Mousses and Souffles

Hot or cold, the airy and flamboyant soufflés and fluffy mousses are the most ethereal of this dessert genre.

Chocolate Mousse (eggless)

Serves 8

INGREDIENTS

250 gms	*Dark cooking chocolate*
100 gms	*Butter*
4 tbsps	*Powdered Sugar*
½ cup	*Milk*
½ cup	*Cream*
1 tsp	*Gelatine*
1 tsp	*Vanilla essence*
½ cup	*Whipping cream*

To garnish

Whipped cream and chocolate curls

METHOD

Melt chocolate and cream over a pan of boiling water or in microwave on high for one minute. Mix gelatine in milk and melt it over medium heat. Set aside to cool. Beat butter and sugar in a medium bowl until creamy. Add melted chocolate and cream along with vanilla. Beat this over a bowl of ice. Add gelatine mixture in a thin stream. Beat until the mixture is thick. Remove the bowl from ice and fold in the whipped cream. Spoon this into individual stemmed glasses or six bowls and refrigerate for one hour. Garnish with whipped cream and chocolate curls. Serve cold.

Orange-Chocolate Mousse

Serves 4-6

INGREDIENTS

5 gms	*China grass or 3 tsps of gelatine*
5 tbsps	*Orange juice*
½ cup	*Sugar*
¼ cup	*Cocoa powder*
¼ cup	*Water*
2 tbsps	*Milk*
1 tsp	*Orange essence*
¼ tsp	*Freshly grated orange peel*
1 cup	*Whipping cream*

METHOD

Soak china grass or gelatine in orange juice and let it stand for one minute. Cook over a slow flame till the china grass dissolves and becomes a transparent liquid. Take it off the heat and cool it by stirring continuously. In a small saucepan, combine sugar, cocoa and water. Cook over low heat, stirring constantly, until slightly thickened. Remove from heat, add china grass mixture and stir until dissolved. Blend in the milk and vanilla. Cool. In a small mixer bowl, combine whipped cream and orange peel. Beat until stiff. Gradually add chocolate mixture to the whipped cream. Spoon into dessert dishes and refrigerate for one hour. Serve chilled.

Mexican Chocolate Mousse

Serves 8

INGREDIENTS

200 gms	*Semi-sweet chocolate, cut into pieces*
¾ cup	*Powdered sugar*
¾ cup	*Fresh cream*
1 cup	*Whipping cream*
1 tbsp	*Rum (optional)*
1 tsp	*Vanilla essence*

To Garnish

¼ cup	*Slivered almonds, toasted*
Sprigs of fresh mint	

METHOD

In a heavy saucepan combine chocolate, sugar and fresh cream. Stir over low heat until completely melted. Set aside to cool. Add rum (if using) and vanilla. Whip the remaining cream until soft peaks form. Fold melted and cooled chocolate into whipped cream. Spoon into dessert bowl or individual dessert glasses. Cover and chill in the refrigerator for four hours or until ready to serve. Garnish with almonds and mint sprigs.

Note: Melt chocolate, sugar and fresh cream in a bowl in the microwave on high for three-four minutes. Stir after two minutes. Remove and cool. Proceed as above.

Double-Layer Chocolate Mousse

Serves 6-8

INGREDIENTS

12-14 pieces	*Oreo cookies, cream removed and powdered*
2-3 tbsps	*Powdered sugar*
For the Chocolate Layer	
200 gms	*Dark cooking chocolate*
½ cup	*Powdered sugar*
½ cup	*Fresh cream*
1 cup	*Whipping cream*
1 tsp	*Vanilla essence*
1½ tbsps	*Rum (optional)*
For the White Layer	
200 gms	*Cream cheese, softened*
½ cup	*Powdered sugar*
1 cup	*Whipping cream*
1 tsp	*Vanilla essence*

To Garnish

Chocolate shavings and whipped cream

METHOD

Mix Oreo cookie crumbs with sugar and set aside.

For the chocolate mixture

Combine chocolate with sugar and half a cup of cream and melt over boiling water. Stir until completely melted. Set aside to cool. Add rum (if using). Beat the cream over ice until stiff. Fold into the chocolate mixture.

For the white layer

Beat cream cheese with vanilla and sugar in a small bowl until fluffy. Beat the cream over ice until stiff. Fold into the cheese mixture. Set aside.

Take a transparent glass bowl and sprinkle half the Oreo crumbs at the bottom. Spread chocolate mixture over it. Smoothen the top. Sprinkle remaining cookie crumbs and then the cream cheese mixture. Chill in the refrigerator for one hour. Garnish with chocolate shavings and whipped cream and serve.

Kahlua Chocolate Mousse

Serves 6-8

INGREDIENTS

250 gms	*Dark cooking chocolate*
125 gms	*Butter*
4	*Eggs*
4 tbsps	*Powdered sugar*
100 gms	*Fresh cream*
2 tbsps	*Kahlua*

METHOD

Melt the chocolate in a medium bowl over a saucepan filled with simmering water. Separate the eggs: whites in a bigger bowl and yolks in a smaller bowl. Cut the butter into small chunks. When the chocolate has melted, whisk until smooth. Remove the bowl from the heat, add butter and whisk until all the lumps have melted. Add egg yolks. Continue to whisk, until smooth. With dry beaters, whisk egg whites, adding sugar slowly as the egg whites become stiff, but not dry. Scrape the chocolate mixture into a large bowl and fold in the whites. Whip the cream with Kahlua until stiff and fold into the mousse. Pour this into a big bowl or into individual stem glasses and set for four hours or probably overnight. Decorate.

Three-Layered Toblerone Mousse

Serves 6-8

INGREDIENTS

100 gms (each)	*Three Toblerone bars, (regular, dark and white)*
¾ cup	*Sugar*
¾ cup	*Fresh cream*
2 cups	*Whipping cream*
1½ tbsps	*Rum (optional)*
1½ tsps	*Vanilla essence*

To Garnish

Chocolate shavings and whipped cream

METHOD

Combine each chocolate with one-fourth cup of sugar and one-fourth cup of cream (each) in three separate stainless steel bowls and melt over boiling water. Stir until completely melted. Set them aside to cool. Add rum (if using), half a tablespoon to each mixture and vanilla, half a teaspoon to each mixture. Beat the cream over ice until stiff. Fold in two-third cup of cream to each chocolate mixture. Take a transparent glass bowl and layer first the white then the light and lastly the dark chocolate mixture. Chill in the refrigerator for one hour. Garnish with chocolate shavings and whipped cream before serving.

Kahlua Chocolate Mousse

Three Layered Toblerone Mousse

Crème Brulée

Crème Brulée

Serves 8

INGREDIENTS

3 cups	*Thick cream*
6	*Egg yolks*
⅓ cup	*Powdered sugar*
1 tsp	*Vanilla essence*
⅓ cup	*Light brown sugar*

METHOD

Heat cream in a heavy saucepan until bubbles form around the edge. In a double boiler pan, beat egg yolks with sugar until thick and light in colour. Gradually stir in the cream. Continue stirring over hot water until the mixture coats the metal spoon. Add the vanilla. Strain the custard into a four cup-sized shallow dish. Refrigerate for eight hours or overnight. Just before serving, sprinkle brown sugar evenly. Set the dish in a pan filled with ice cubes. Place it under a grill just until the sugar melts slightly and caramelizes. It will form a crust. Alternately you can burn the top of cream, using a gourmet torch.

Variations

Chocolate crème brûlée: Mix 150 gms of dark cooking chocolate to boiled cream and make it the same way as the classic crème brûlée.

Peach or strawberry crème brule: Combine one cup of chopped peaches, two tablespoons of brown sugar and one-fourth teaspoon of nutmeg in a bowl. Line a shallow baking dish with this mixture and pour prepared custard over it. Proceed as per the classic crème brûlée recipe.

Chocolate Soufflé

Serves 6.

INGREDIENTS:

2 cups	*Milk*
5 tbsps	*Sugar*
6 tbsps	*Custard powder*
2 tbsps	*Cocoa powder*
1 tsp	*Vanilla essence*
2 ½ tbsps	*Gelatine*
3 tbsps	*Powdered sugar*
1 cup	*Water*
300 gms	*Fresh cream*
5 tbsps	*Powdered sugar*

METHOD

Combine the milk and sugar in a pan and heat. Dissolve the custard powder and cocoa in a little cold milk separately. Add this to the hot milk and stir until thick. Remove from heat and cool. Add the vanilla essence. Mix the gelatine and sugar in a pan with water and put it on the gas to melt. When it is transparent and boiling, take it off and beat it over ice until it resembles cream. Pour the fresh cream into a stainless steel bowl, and beat over ice at a slow speed. Add the sugar, gradually, until the mixture is stiff. Be careful not to curdle the cream. Keep aside half a cup of cream for decoration. Place a big bowl on ice. Add the cooled custard, cream and beaten gelatine. Stir often, scraping the sides until the soufflé becomes thick. Pour into a serving bowl and chill for at least two-four hours.

Mocha Soufflé

Serves 6

INGREDIENTS

2 cups	*Milk*
5 tbsps	*Sugar*
6 tbsps	*Custard powder*
3 tbsps	*Cocoa powder*
1 tsp	*Vanilla essence*
2 ½ tbsps	*Gelatine*
3 tbsps	*Powdered sugar*
2 tbsps	*Instant coffee powder*
1 cup	*Water*
300 gms	*Whipping cream*
5 tbsps	*Powdered sugar*

METHOD

Combine the milk and sugar in a pan and heat. Dissolve the custard powder and cocoa in a little cold milk separately, and add this to the hot milk, stir until thick. Remove from heat and cool. Add the vanilla essence. Mix the gelatin and sugar in a pan with water and put it on the gas to melt. When it is transparent and boiling, take it off and beat it over ice until it looks like cream. Pour the cream into a stainless steel bowl, put it over ice and beat at a slow speed. Add the sugar, a little at a time until stiff. Be careful not to curdle the cream. Keep aside half a cup of cream for decoration. Place a big bowl on ice. Add the cooled custard, cream and beaten gelatin. Stir often, scraping the sides until the soufflé becomes thick. Pour into a serving bowl and chill for at least two-four hours.

Choco-Berry Bavarian Cream

Serves 8-10

INGREDIENTS

1 cup	*Sliced fresh strawberries, mashed with little sugar*
4½ tsps	*Gelatine powder*
½ cup	*Sugar*
1 cup	*Semi-sweet chocolate chips or dark cooking chocolate*
2¼ cups	*Milk*
1 tsp	*Vanilla*
1 cup	*Whipping cream*

For Strawberry Cream

1 cup	*Whipping cream*
1 tsp	*Vanilla essence*

To Garnish

1-2 sliced strawberries

METHOD

Drain mashed strawberries; reserve three-fourth cup of syrup. Sprinkle gelatine over this and set aside. Refrigerate drained strawberries. In a medium saucepan, stir together sugar, chocolate chips and half a cup of milk. Cook over low heat, stirring constantly, until mixture is smooth and very hot. Add gelatine mixture and continue stirring until gelatine is dissolved. Remove from heat, add remaining milk and vanilla. Pour into a metal bowl and refrigerate, stirring occasionally, until mixture is thick. Beat whipping cream until stiff and fold it into the chocolate mixture. Pour into an oiled five-six cup mould. Refrigerate until firm. Unmould. Pipe strawberry cream and garnish with sliced strawberries.

For Strawberry Cream

In a small mixer bowl, beat whipping cream and vanilla together until stiff. Fold in mashed strawberries. Fill this in a piping bag and garnish.

Chocolate Zabaglione

Serves 4

INGREDIENTS

200 gms	*Mascarpone cheese*
2	*Egg yolks*
¼ cup	*Marsala Wine (each) powdered sugar and whipping cream*
3 tsps	*Cocoa mixed with 2 tbsps of hot water*
1 tsp	*Chocolate-flavoured liqueur or vanilla essence*

To Serve

Almond biscotti

METHOD

Beat egg yolks, marsala and sugar until light. Cook over a pan of hot water until thick. Add cooled cocoa mixture and continue cooking, stirring constantly. Remove from fire and add Mascarpone cheese. Cool this mixture over a bowl of ice. Whip the cream until it forms soft peaks. Add chocolate liqueur or vanilla. Fold into the cocoa mixture. Pour into individual glasses and either serve at room temperature or chill. Serve with almond biscotti.

Orange and Lemon Terrine

Serves 6-8

INGREDIENTS

4½ cups	*Freshly squeezed orange juice*
1 cup	*Sweet lime juice*
1 cup	*Fresh cream*
Grated rind of 3 lemons	
⅓ cup	*Lemon juice*
½ cup	*Sugar*
4 tsps	*Gelatine mixed with ½ cup orange juice*
3	*Oranges, peeled and segmented*
2 tbsps	*Orange liqueur (optional)*

To Garnish

Fresh mint leaves

METHOD

In a saucepan, heat together two cups of orange juice, one cup of sweet lime juice, one-third cup of lemon juice, grated rind of lemon and half a cup of sugar. Bring to a boil and add gelatine mixture, stirring constantly. Cook until gelatine is dissolved. Remove from stove and cool over a pan of ice. Stir frequently. Make sure it does not set. Arrange peeled oranges at the bottom of six inches by nine inches loaf tin. Chill. When the mixture begins to thicken, add beaten cream and whisk until well-blended. Pour this in a prepared tin, cover and freeze it. Heat the balance of two cups of orange juice and one-fourth cup of sugar, on a medium flame, till it is reduced to half. Remove from the stove and cool. Add orange liqueur (if using). Unmould the terrine onto a serving plate, cut in slices and pour the orange sauce all around. Garnish with fresh mint leaves.

Raspberry-Tangerine Mousse

Serves 4-6

INGREDIENTS

1 cup	*Tangerine juice*
1 cup	*Segments*
1½ tbsps	*Gelatine*
½ cup	*Powdered sugar*
4 tbsps	*Rasberry syrup*
1 tbsp	*Lemon juice*
1½ cups	*Whipping cream*

To Garnish

A few tangerine slices

METHOD

Soak gelatine in three tablespoons of cold water and cook on a low flame until dissolved. Add tangerine and lemon juice. Sieve. Cool over a bowl of ice. When it begins to thicken, remove and add orange segments, raspberry syrup and sugar. Use a beater to mix the mixture. Whip the cream to soft peaks and fold it into the mixture. Pour this in a serving bowl or individual dessert glasses and chill. Garnish before serving.

Orange Soufflé

Serves 6

INGREDIENTS

2 cups	*Orange segments*
2 cups	*Milk*
5 tbsps	*Sugar*
6 tsps	*Custard powder*
¾ tsp	*Orange essence*
2 ½ tbsps	*Gelatine OR*
5 gms	*China grass*
1 tbsp	*Sugar*
1 cup	*Orange juice*
2 tbsps	*Lemon juice*
300 gms	*Fresh cream*
5 tbsps	*Powdered sugar*

To Garnish

A few orange slices

Whipped cream

METHOD

Combine the milk and five tablespoon of sugar in a saucepan and heat. Dissolve the custard powder in a little cold milk and add to the hot milk. Stir until thick. Remove from the heat and cool. Mix in the orange essence. Then mix together the chopped China grass or gelatine and one tablespoon of sugar and add to the orange juice. Boil on a slow flame and add lemon juice. When the china grass or gelatine is completely dissolved, remove from heat and beat over a bowl of ice cubes with an electric beater until fluffy and creamy. Beat the fresh cream in a chilled stainless steel bowl. Gradually add five tablespoons of powdered sugar. Keep beating over the ice until stiff. Take a big bowl and place it over the ice cubes. Mix in the cooled custard, cream, beaten orange mixture and orange segments. Mix well. Place it over ice, scraping the sides until the soufflé becomes thick. Pour this in a serving bowl and set for about three-four hours or overnight in the refrigerator. Just before serving, pipe some cream and arrange sliced oranges on top.

Strawberry Soufflé

Serves 6

INGREDIENTS

2 cups	*Chopped strawberries*
2 cups	*Milk*
5 tbsps	*Sugar*
6 tsps	*Custard powder*
¾ tsp	*Strawberry essence*
2½ tbsps	*Gelatine*
1 tbsp	*Sugar*
1 cup	*Strawberry pulp and water*
2 tbsps	*Lemon juice*
300 gms	*Fresh cream*
5 tbsps	*Powdered sugar*

To Garnish

A few strawberry slices and whipped cream

METHOD

Combine the milk and five tablespoons of sugar in a saucepan and heat. Dissolve the custard powder in a little cold milk and add to the hot milk. Stir until thick. Remove from the heat and cool. Mix in the strawberry essence. Mix together the gelatine and one tablespoon of sugar and add this to the strawberry pulp. Boil on a slow flame and add lemon juice. When the gelatine is completely dissolved, remove from heat and beat it over a bowl of ice cubes with an electric beater until fluffy and creamy. Beat the fresh cream in a chilled stainless steel bowl; gradually add five tablespoons of powdered sugar. Keep beating over the ice until stiff. Take a large bowl and place it over the ice cubes. Mix in the cooled custard, cream, beaten gelatine mixture and chopped strawberries. Mix well. Place over ice, scraping the sides until the soufflé becomes thick. Pour this in a serving bowl and set for about three-four hours or overnight in the refrigerator. Just before serving, pipe some cream and arrange sliced strawberries on top.

Strawberry Mousse

Serves 6-8

INGREDIENTS

3	*Eggs*
2	*Eggs yolks*
100 gms	*Powdered sugar, sieved*
300 gms	*Double cream*
225 gms	*Strawberries*
2 tbsps	*Brandy or lemon juice*
15 gms	*Gelatine mixed with five tablespoons of liquid*

To Garnish

Sliced strawberries and whipped cream

METHOD

Beat the whole eggs and the yolks in a big bowl at high speed for at least five minutes. Then add the sugar spoon by spoon, and continue to beat for seven more minutes. Transfer this mixture to another big bowl. Beat the cream to a thick consistency. Liquidize the cleaned strawberries with icing sugar and brandy or lemon juice. Reduce this mixture on the stove to 150 ml and then cool it. Combine the cream with the strawberry mixture and whip it enough to merge with the egg mixture. Fold it into the egg mixture in circular movements. Fold in the gelatine at the end and pour the mixture into a one and a half litre sized big bowl or small individual bowls and chill in the refrigerator. Garnish before serving with slices of strawberries and whipped cream.

Peach Mousse

Serves 6-8

INGREDIENTS

2 cups	*Chopped peaches*
1 cup	*Powdered sugar*
1 tbsp	*Gelatine*
¼ cup	*Cold water*
2 tbsps	*Lemon juice*
2 cups	*Whipping cream*

To Garnish

Peach slices and Mint leaves

METHOD

Mash the peaches and sieve. Soak gelatine in water and cook until completely dissolved. Cool. Mix fruit pulp, sugar, lemon juice and gelatine mixture in a bowl and chill over a bowl of ice. When this begins to thicken, whip the cream to soft peaks and fold into the peach mixture. Continue chilling over a bowl of ice. Either transfer it to a serving bowl or fill it in a piping bag and pipe in a swirl in small glasses. Chill until ready to serve. Garnish with peach slices and mint leaves.

Hazelnut Mousse

Serves 6

INGREDIENTS

100 gms	*Hazelnuts, toasted and powdered*
3 large	*Eggs*
½ cup	*Powdered sugar*
1 tbsp	*Vanilla essence or hazelnut liqueur*
200 gms	*Fresh cream, beaten*

To Garnish

2-3 halved hazelnuts

Whipped Cream

METHOD

Beat the eggs on high speed until light. Add sugar gradually and continue beating until the mixture has a ribbon-like consistency. Fold the nuts into the cream with a metal spoon. Fold this mixture very gently into the egg mixture. Add vanilla or the liqueur. Pour this into a six cup-sized serving bowl or six individual bowls. Set in the refrigerator for two-four hours. Garnish with nuts and whipped cream before serving.

Eggless Version

Replace three eggs with one cup of milk mixed with three tablespoons of custard powder.

Boil this with sugar. In another small pan, mix one tablespoon of gelatine powder with one-fourth cup of water, boil and cool over ice, beating continuously. Mix the milk and gelatine mixture with the beater. Fold in the nuts, vanilla and beaten cream. Pour into a serving bowl and set in the refrigerator. Garnish with nuts and whipped cream.

Cookies and Confectionaries

Who stole the cookie from the cookie jar? Sugar and spice and all things nice, that's what cookies are made of! These universal favourite little cakes... Cookies and confectioneries are ideal for gift giving, perfect for countless occasions, from casual nibbles, picnics and box lunches to elegant tea accompaniments and dinner finales.

Fudgy Bonbons

Makes 2-2½ dozen

INGREDIENTS

2 cups	*Chopped dark cooking chocolate*
¼ cup	*Butter*
1 tin (400gms)	*Condensed milk*
2 cups	*Plain flour (sieved)*
½ cup	*Finely chopped nuts*
1 tsp	*Vanilla essence*
30 pieces	*Small marshmallows*
To Garnish	
¾ cup	*Icing sugar*
½ tbsp	*Corn flour*
2 tbsps	*Water*
2-3 drops	*Flavouring*

METHOD

In a medium saucepan mix chocolate and butter. Cook and stir over low heat until the chocolate has melted and become smooth. Add condensed milk to it. Mix well. In a medium bowl, combine flour, nuts, chocolate mixture and vanilla. Mix well. Shape one tablespoon of dough around one marshmallow, covering it completely. Place them one inch apart from each other on ungreased cookie sheet. Bake at 350°F for 6 to 8 minutes. Do not over bake. The cookies will be soft and appear shiny, but will become firm as they cool. Remove from the cookie sheet and place them on a rack.

For Garnish

Gently heat icing sugar, corn flour, water and flavoring until smooth. Drizzle over cookies. Store in an airtight container.

Pineapple Barfi
(Pineapple Sweet)

Makes 10-12 pieces

INGREDIENTS

1 cup	*Thickened milk (khoya)*
1 cup	*Cottage cheese*
⅓ cup	*Finely chopped pineapple*
½ cup	*Powdered sugar*

A few strands of saffron, mixed with milk

To garnish

Silver foil

METHOD

Grate khoya and heat in small frying pan until a little ghee separates out. Cool. Similarly grate and heat cottage cheese in a pan until dry. Cool. Mix together khoya and cottage cheese with sugar. Rub well to get soft mixture. Add saffron and mix well. Spread half the mixture in a tray in rectangular shape. Sprinkle pineapple pieces over this and cover with the remaining half of khoya-cottage cheese mixture. Press gently to give a neat surface. Cut into diamond shape and arrange each piece on a paper cup. Serve either at room temperature or cold. Alternately make small balls of khoya-cottage cheese mixture and press to form a disc. Stuff a few pieces of pineapple in each one and give it either round or oblong shape. Place them on paper cups.

Peanut Butter Crisps

Makes 2½ dozens

INGREDIENTS

½ cup	*Butter, soften and divided*
½ cup	*Powdered sugar*
1 large	*Egg*
1 tsp	*Corn flour mixed with two tablespoons of water*
¾ cup	*Peanut butter chips (Reese's)*
1 cup	*Plain flour*
1 tsp	*Baking soda*

A pinch of salt

METHOD

In a large bowl beat one-third of cup butter and one-third of cup of sugar until light. Add egg, corn syrup and vanilla. Melt remaining butter and add peanut butter chips. Blend into butter mixture. Mix flour, baking soda and salt in a bowl. Add this to the same mixture. Blend well. Refrigerate this dough for one hour. Preheat the oven to 350°F. Roll out the dough into one inch balls; roll in sugar. Place on ungreased cookie sheet. Bake 10-12 minutes or until golden brown around the edges. Cool slightly; Remove from cookie sheet and cool on wire rack. Cool completely.

Chocolate Dipped Dates

Makes 12 to 15

INGREDIENTS

12-15	*Large black dates. deseeded*
12-15 pieces	*Blanched whole almonds*
100 gms	*White chocolate*
100 gms	*Dark chocolate*
12-15	*Paper cups*

METHOD

Melt both the chocolate separately over a pan of hot water. Remove and set aside to cool. Stuff each date with one piece of almond. Holding one end of the stuffed date dip the other end into melted chocolate. Put it on the wire rack till it dries out completely. Repeat the same for the remaining dates, dip half the date in white chocolate and the other half in the dark chocolate. Arrange them in individual paper cups when completely dry and store in an airtight box.

Chocolate and Pistachio Clusters

Makes 20

INGREDIENTS

125 gms	*Shelled and toasted pistachios*
60 ml	*Water*
150 gms	*Sugar*
1½ tbsps	*Butter*
¼ tsp	*Soda bi-carbonate*
200 gms	*Semi-sweet cooking chocolate*

METHOD

Line the baking sheet with greaseproof paper and butter it lightly. In a heavy saucepan, mix sugar and water. Bring it to a boil without stirring. Cook until golden in colour. Remove from stove and add pistachios immediately. Stir in soda and butter using a wooden spoon. Spoon 20 small clusters on a buttered baking sheet and set aside to cool. Melt the chocolate over a pan of hot water. Stir until smooth. Set aside to cool. Line another baking sheet and spoon dollops of chocolate onto it, as many as the nut clusters. Gently loosen the clusters and push them into the pool of melted chocolate, in a way that the chocolate shows through from the edges. Set in a cool place. Peel off and store in an airtight container.

Note : You can replace pistachios for toasted and chopped almonds or mixed nuts for nut clusters.

Chocolate Boxes

Makes 16

INGREDIENTS

1 8" square	*Chocolate sponge cake (recipe on page 20)*
1 box (68 pieces)	*Lindt thins chocolates*
For the Icing	
100 gms	*Butter*
250 gms	*Icing sugar*
2 tbsps	*Milk*
½ tsp	*Vanilla essence*
2 tbsps	*Cocoa powder mixed with 1 tbsp of water (optional)*

METHOD

For the Icing

Beat butter and half of the icing sugar in a bowl until smooth. Add remaining sugar with milk, vanilla and cocoa mixture (if using). Beat thoroughly until smooth.

Split the sponge cake in half horizontally and sandwich the halves with one-fourth of the icing. Cut into 16 squares. Spread more icing round the sides. Press a lindt chocolate square onto each side to form a box. Place remaining icing in a piping bag fitted with a fluted nozzle and pipe rosettes on top of each box. Cut the remaining chocolate squares into triangles and place on each box.

Chocolate Boxes

Chocolate and Pistachio Clusters

Chocolate and Cream Cheese Pizza

Chocolate Fudge Brownies

Chocolate-Cream Cheese Pizza

Serves 6-8

INGREDIENTS

12 small	*Pizza bases, trimmed from top*
½ cup	*Philadelphia cream cheese*
3-4 tbsps	*Icing sugar*
½ cup	*Chopped chocolate*
½ tsp	*Vanilla essence*
¼ cup	*Sliced nuts*

Melted butter to grease the dough

To Garnish

Glossy chocolate sauce (recipe on page 20)

METHOD

Brush the pizza bases with melted butter and place them on a baking tray. In a small, bowl mix together cream cheese, icing sugar and vanilla essence. Spread this mixture on each pizza base evenly. Top it with chopped chocolate and sliced nuts. Lightly brush melted butter on the nuts and bake it in an hot oven for five-seven minutes. Remove and dribble little chocolate over each one. Serve hot.

Chocolate Fudge Brownies

Makes 16 pieces

INGREDIENTS

½ cup	*Plain sifted flour*
¼ tsp	*Baking powder*
¼ tsp	*Salt*
½ cup	*Butter (softened)*
½ cup	*Sugar (powdered)*
½ cup	*Brown sugar*
2	*Eggs*
250 gms	*Unsweetened cooking chocolate (melted)*
½ tsp	*Vanilla essence*
1 cup	*Chopped walnuts*
To Sprinkle	
1 tbsp	*Sugar (powdered)*
To Serve	
100 gms	*Fresh cream*
3 tbsps	*Powdered sugar*

A pinch of cinnamon powder

METHOD

Pre-heat the oven to 325°F. Lightly grease an 8" x 8" x 2" inch baking pan. Sift flour with baking powder and salt. In a small bowl, beat the butter with the sugar at high speed in an electric mixture till fluffy. Beat in the eggs, one at a time, until very light. Then beat in the melted chocolate and vanilla.

At low speed, blend in the flour mixture just until combined. Stir in the nuts. Turn into prepared pan and spread evenly. Bake for 30 minutes. Cool for 10 minutes. With a sharp knife, cut into squares. Let it cool completely in the pan, and then remove and arrange them onto a serving plate. Sprinkle with one tablespoon of the powdered sugar and serve with fresh cream.

For the Cream

In a chilled stainless steel bowl, beat cream at a low speed and add sugar, spoon-by-spoon, along with cinnamon until it forms soft peaks. Chill it in the refrigerator till ready to serve.

Date and Almond Sandwich Cookies

Serves 4-6

INGREDIENTS

½ cup	*Pitted and chopped dates*
⅓ cup	*Roasted and chopped almonds*
½ cup	*Cream cheese*
1-2 tbsps	*Honey or powdered sugar*
¼ tsp	*Powdered cinnamon*
16 pieces	*Sweet cookies or fruit cake slices*

METHOD

Beat the cream cheese with cinnamon and sugar or honey until light. Fold in chopped dates and almonds. Sandwich two cookies or two slices of fruit cake with this mixture. Serve at room temperature.

Stuffed Dates

Makes 14 pieces

INGREDIENTS

12-14 pieces	*Black Dates*
2 tbsps	*Melted butter*
¼ cup	*Cream Cheese*
2-3 tbsps	*Icing Sugar*
½ tsp	*Vanilla essence*
6-7 pieces	*Almonds, blanched and halved*

METHOD

Slit the dates vertically from the centre. Remove seeds and strings, it any. Brush them with melted butter. In a small bowl beat cream cheese with icing sugar and vanilla. Fill this in the piping bag mixture, slightly showing on the rim. Press halved almonds on each one, length wise. Arrange on a serving plate or in paper cups. Serve at room temperature.

Brandy Snaps

Make approx. 20 cookies

INGREDIENTS

For the Cookies

¾ cup	Flour
1 tsp	Ground ginger
½ cup	Butter
4 tbsps	Golden syrup
½ cup	Caster sugar
2 tsps	Brandy (optional)
A pinch of salt	
Grated rind of 1 lemon	

For the Filling

3 cups	Cream
3 tbsps	Icing sugar
1 tbsp	Brandy
75 gms	Bitter-sweet chocolate, finely chopped (optional)

METHOD

For the Cookies: Preheat the oven to 325°F. Lightly butter the two baking sheets and grease a few moulds or bowls. In a medium-sized bowl, mix together the flour, ginger and salt. In a heavy saucepan, combine butter, golden syrup and sugar. Simmer over a medium flame, stirring with a wooden spoon until the butter has melted and the mixture is smooth. Remove from heat. Using a whisk add the flour mixture into the golden syrup mixture until smooth. Do not over mix. Whisk in the brandy. Drop the batter using level tablespoonfuls onto the prepared baking sheets. Leave four inch space between two cookies. Use a rubber spatula to level the top of the batter. Bake for 8-10 minutes. Cool the cookies on a wire rack for one-two minutes, until the shape holds. Lift the cookies one at a time. Place face down and roll up around the mould. Let it sit for 30 seconds and then gently remove from the mould and completely cool on a wire-rack. Repeat the same process to make the remaining cookies. If the cookies become too firm, return them to the oven to slightly soften them.

For the Filling: In a chilled stainless steel bowl, beat the cream with sugar and brandy until stiff peaks form. Fold in the chocolate (it using) and chill until use. Fill the cookies with this cream filling just before serving.

Date and Almond Sandwich Cookies

Brandy Snaps

Hawaiian Pineapple Pastry

hocolate-chip Cookies

Hawaiian Pineapple Pastry

Makes 10-12 rounds

INGREDIENTS

For Pineapple Pastry

1 small can	*Pineapple slices*
¼ kg	*Plain sponge cake*
2 tbsps	*Mixed fruit jam*
200 gms	*Fresh cream*
4-6 tbsps	*Powdered sugar*

To Garnish

Glaze cherries

For Short Crust Pastry

225 gms	*Plain flour, sieved*
115 gms	*Butter, cold*
2-3 tbsps	*Cold water*
A pinch of salt	

METHOD

For Short Crust Pastry

Mix together plain flour with salt and rub butter into it. Rub this into the flour with your fingertips and add ice cold water to make a soft dough. Cover and chill for half an hour before use. Roll out thin short crust pastries and cut out even rounds with a pastry cutter. The size should be similar to the pineapple pieces. Prick the pastries with a fork and bake it on an un-greased baking sheet in a hot oven 220°C for 10-12 minutes. Cool the pastries.

For the Pineapple Pastry

Drain the pineapple slices and cut each into two pieces horizontally. Reserve the syrup. Apply a thin layer of jam over each pastry. Slice the cake thinly (about half a cm thick) and cut out the rounds with the same cutter as the pastry. Soak each slice with the reserved syrup. Beat the cream with sugar in a stainless steel bowl until thick. Take one pastry round, place one slice of cake over it, spoon a little cream, put another slice over it and finally top it up with a pineapple slice and a cherry. Chill thoroughly and serve.

Chocolate-chip Cookies

Makes 36-40 cookies

INGREDIENTS

½ cup	*Butter*
⅓ cup	*Powdered sugar*
⅓ cup	*Brown sugar*
1	*Beaten egg or one-fourth cup of cream*
1 ¼ cups	*Plain flour, sieved*
½ tsp	*Baking and*
½ tsp	*Soda bi carbonate*
1 cup	*Chocolate chips*
1 tsp	*Vanilla essence*
¼ tsp	*Salt*
½ cup	*Chopped nuts*

METHOD

Mix thoroughly the butter, both types of sugar, vanilla and egg or cream. Stir in the remaining ingredients. Add one-fourth cup of additional flour for rounder cookies. Drop dough in rounded spoonfuls, two inches apart on the ungreased baking sheet. Bake for 8-10 minutes or until light brown. Cool slightly before removing from the sheet. Cool on a wire rack. Fill in an airtight jar.

Chocolate-Walnut Fudge

Makes ½ kg fudge

INGREDIENTS

450 gms	*Castor sugar*
150 ml (¼ pint)	*Milk*
100 gms	*Plain cooking chocolate*
50 gms	*Maple syrup or honey*
150 gms	*Butter*
100 gms	*Chopped walnuts*

METHOD

Grease an eight x six inch tin. Mix together sugar, milk, chocolate and honey or maple syrup in a large thick saucepan over gentle heat. Stir constantly until the sugar has dissolved. Bring to a boil until it reaches the softball stage. Remove from heat, add the butter and leave to cool for about five minutes, without stirring. Then beat the mixture until thick, creamy and begins to grain. Add all the chopped nuts at once and stir with a wooden spoon until they are mixed into the fudge. Immediately pour this mixture into the greased tin. Leave until it is completely cold. Then cut the fudge into squares and remove from the tin and store in an airtight container.

Cocoa-Nut Crunchies

Makes approx. 650 gms

INGREDIENTS

¾ cup	Butter
1 cup	Sugar
⅓ cup	Cocoa
2 tbsps	Corn flour
4 tbsps	Water
¾ cup	Toasted and chopped nuts

METHOD

Melt butter in a heavy saucepan; stir in sugar, cocoa, corn flour and water. Cook over medium heat, stirring constantly until the syrup, when dropped into cold water separates into threads. Remove from heat; stir in nuts and immediately spread the mixture evenly (about one-fourth inch thick) on a greased cookie sheet. Cool on a rack or refrigerate until cold. Remove from sheet; break into serving size pieces. Store in a tightly covered container in the refrigerator.

Italian Nut Balls

Makes 36 balls

INGREDIENTS

½ cup	Softened butter
1/3 cup	Powdered sugar
2-3 tbsps	Thick cream
¾ tsp	Vanilla essence
1 cup	Plain flour
½ tsp	Salt
½ tsp	Baking powder
¾ cup	Chopped pistachio nuts
½ cup	Orange marmalade

To Serve

Cinnamon ice-cream

Whipped cream

METHOD

Cream butter, sugar and vanilla with an electric beater until fluffy. Sift flour with salt and baking powder. Add this to butter mixture alternating with cream. Form into small balls, using about half a tablespoon of dough for each. Dip each one in little milk and then roll in the nuts. Place them on a buttered tray and make a slight depression in the centre. Bake it in a hot oven at 300°F for 20-25 minutes. Remove from the oven, fill the marmalade in the depression and serve warm with cinnamon ice-cream or whipped cream.

Cashew Puri Sandwich
(Cashewnut Cakes Sandwich with Saffron Cream)

Makes 8 sandwiches

INGREDIENTS

16 pieces	*Coin sized cashew puries (purchased)*
1/4 cup	*Powdered pistachios*
1/4 cup	*Almonds*
2-3 tbsps	*Thick sugar syrup*
1/2 tsp	*Powdered cardamom*
2 tbsps	*Thick cream*
For Saffron Cream	
1/4 cup	*Butter*
1/2 cup	*Icing sugar*

A few stands of saffron dissolved in little milk

METHOD

Slightly warm cashew puries in the oven. In a small bowl, mix together powdered nuts, cardamom, cream and sugar syrup. Take two puries and sandwich them with one tablespoon of nut mixture. Set aside.

For Saffron Cream

In a small bowl beat butter and icing sugar until light. Add dissolved saffron and beat again. Fill this cream in an icing syringe and pipe small stars on each sandwich. Serve at room temperature.

Note : Cashew puri is a Indian speciality. It is a small disc made with powdered nuts and sugar. If looks like small cookies.

Cookie Cheesecake

Makes 18-20 cookies

INGREDIENTS

12-14 pieces	*Chocolate cookies, halved, cream removed*
1 cup	*Cream cheese*
½ cup	*Condensed milk*
½ cup	*Whipping cream*
2 tsps	*Gelatine, mixed with three tbsps of strong coffee*
1 tsp	*Camp coffee or vanilla essence*
18-20	*Paper cups*

To garnish

Grated chocolate or silver balls

METHOD

Slightly toast the halved cookies and place each one in individual paper cups. In a medium bowl, beat cream cheese with condensed milk until light. Whip the cream in a separate bowl until stiff. Fold it into the cheese mixture. Cook gelatine powder and coffee on a slow flame till it has melted. Cool. Add camp coffee essence and pour this liquid in a thin stream into the cheese mixture. Do this over a bowl of ice cubes. When the mixture begins to set, fill it in a piping bag and freeze for five-ten minutes to harden. Pipe the cheesecake mixture over the cookies and garnish each one with grated chocolate or silver balls. Chill the cookies until ready to serve.

Date and Almond Squares

Makes 30 pieces

INGREDIENTS

For the Date Mixture

450 gms	*Dates, chopped coarsely*
8 tbsps	*Brown sugar, powdered*
1 tbsp	*Flour*
1 cup	*Water*
1 tsp	*Vanilla essence*

For the Pastry

1 cup	*Plain flour*
1 tsp	*Soda sieved together*
A pinch of salt	
1 cup	*Brown sugar, powdered*
1 cup	*Butter, melted*
1 cup	*Almonds, powdered*

Grease a 9" x 12" tray with butter

METHOD

For the Date mixture

Mix together dates, sugar, flour and water in a pan. Cook until thick, stirring occasionally. Take it off the stove, add vanilla, mix well and set aside.

For the Pastry

Add the almonds and sugar to the sieved flour mixture in a bowl and mix well. Add cooled melted butter and mix well to form a soft dough. Divide the pastry in half and spread over the prepared baking tray. Top it up with the date mixture and cover the rest of the pastry. Bake in a pre-heated oven at 180°C for 30 minutes. Cool and cut into even squares.

Almond Cream with Sweet Wontons

Serves 6

INGREDIENTS

For Almond Cream

2 cups	*Milk*
3 tsps	*Custard powder*
3 tbsps	*Sugar*
2 tbsps	*Gelatine, soaked in 4 tbsps of water*
½ tsp	*Vanilla or almond essence*
¼ cup	*Finely chopped almonds*
200 gms	*Fresh cream, whipped with 3 tbsps of powdered sugar*

For the Wontons

10-12	*Wonton wrappers*
1 tsp	*Corn flour mixed with a little water*
3 tbsps	*Finely chopped glaced cherries*
4 tbsps	*Powdered sugar*
Oil for frying	

METHOD

For the Almond Cream

Melt the gelatine on a slow flame till transparent, cool and set aside. In a sauce-pan, mix together milk, sugar and custard powder. Cook on medium heat until thick. Remove from the stove and add the essence, almonds and gelatine mixture. Cool to room temperature and add beaten cream. Pour this into a serving bowl or five-cup size aluminum tin if you wish to unmould. Chill in the refrigerator till it sets.

For the Wontons

Place each wrapper on a board, put half a teaspoon of chopped cherry on each one and fold across opposite ends in a triangle. Seal with corn flour paste. Lift up both the sealed corners and seal them again at the tip to create a wonton shape. Deep fry in hot oil till crisp and drain on a kitchen paper. Sprinkle sugar while still hot. Serve with almond cream.

Note : If you do not want to unmould the pudding, you may reduce the gelatine by one tablespoon.

Almond Shortbreads

Makes 24 pieces

INGREDIENTS

200 gms	*Plain flour, sifted*
50 gms	*Grounded almonds*
125 gms	*Powdered sugar*
175 gms	*Butter*
24 pieces	*Split almonds, blanched*

METHOD

Beat together butter and sugar until light and fluffy. Add flour and almonds to form soft dough. Shape the dough into a rectangular log (6"x 3"x 1½"). Cover and chill for one hour. Cut into one-fourth inch thick slices and place them well apart on baking sheets. Press one split almond into the centre of each and bake in preheated warm oven at 140° C or 275° F for 35 minutes or until pale golden. Cool on a wire rack.

Almond Bisticks

Makes 32 biscuits

INGREDIENTS

200 gms	*Plain flour, sieved*
175 gms	*Butter*
50 gms	*Powdered sugar*
1 tsp	*Vanilla essence*
A pinch of salt	

For the Topping

50 gms	*Castor sugar*
50 gms	*Chopped and toasted almonds*
A pinch of cinnamon	
A little milk to brush	

METHOD

Grease baking sheets. Cream the butter with sugar until light and fluffy. Add the essence, flour and salt and mix well. Refrigerate for about one hour. Gather the mixture into a ball and use hands to a smooth but firm dough. Roll out on a lightly-floured board to a 12 inch x eight inch rectangle. Using a sharp knife, cut into three inches x one inch sticks. Place them slightly apart on a baking sheet. Mix sugar, cinnamon and chopped almonds in a bowl. Brush each stick with little milk and then sprinkle with almond mixture. Bake at 170°C for 15 minutes or until golden brown. Remove from the baking sheet and cool on a wire rack. Store in an airtight jar.

Apple Brownies

Serves 8

INGREDIENTS

½ cup	Butter
1 cup	Powdered brown sugar
1½ cups	Plain flour, sieved
½ tsp	Baking powder,
½ tsp	Baking soda
½ tsp	Salt
½ tsp	Cinnamon
½ cup	Chopped almonds or walnuts
2 medium	Apples, peeled, cored and finely chopped
¼ cup	Thick cream or 1 egg, beaten

METHOD

In a large bowl beat butter and sugar until light. Add beaten egg (if using) or add the cream. Fold in nuts and chopped apples. Mix all the dry ingredients in another bowl and fold them in the butter mixture. Turn the batter into a greased 7x11 baking pan and bake at 350°F or 150°c for 30-35 minutes. Cool and cut into squares, sprinkle with cinnamon sugar and serve warm.

Panaforte
(Spanish Nougat)

Makes 750 gms

INGREDIENTS

200 gms	*Blanched chopped almonds*
300 gms	*Chopped mixed nuts (hazelnut, pistachio, walnut)*
½ cup	*Plain flour*
¼ cup	*Cocoa powder*
2 tsps	*Powdered cinnamon, nutmeg and cloves*
300 gms	*Chopped glaced fruit*
½ cup	*Honey*
¾ cup	*Sugar*

Greased loose bottom tin, 8 inches

To Garnish

Icing sugar

METHOD

Mix nuts, flour, sifted cocoa, powdered spices and glaced fruit in a bowl. Make a toffee with honey and sugar. Cook till the softball stage is reached. Pour this over the dry ingredients and mix with a wooden spoon. As it starts cooling, mix it with hands. Press it into an eight inch greased tin. Bake for 20 minutes at 350°C. Remove from oven and loosen the sides and cool completely in the tin. Remove and sprinkle icing sugar on top. Serve with ice-cream or by itself. Store in an airtight jar. Serve with coffee or as an accompaniment to ice-cream.

Almond Biscotti

Makes 15 cookies

INGREDIENTS

1/4 cup	Fresh cream
1/3 cup	Sugar
4 tbsps	Butter
1/2 cup	Sliced almonds
1/2 cup	Powdered almonds
1/4 cup	Candied orange peel, finely chopped
2 tbsps	Plain flour, sieved with half tsp of baking powder
1 tsp	Vanilla essence

METHOD

In a small saucepan, combine cream, sugar and butter. Place on a stove and bring to a boil gently. Remove from heat and stir in the almonds, orange peel, flour and vanilla essence. Drop one level tablespoon of mixture on a greased baking sheet or in cookie moulds. Bake in a hot oven at 350°F for 10-12 minutes or until the edges are slightly brown. Remove and cool for two minutes and carefully transfer on a wire rack, upside down. Serve with coffee or as an accompaniment to the ice-cream.

Mewavati
(Dry fruit pastries)

Makes 8-10

INGREDIENTS

For the Dough

1 cup — *Plain flour*
1/4 cup — *Semolina*
2 1/2 tbsps — *Hot clarified butter*
Water to bind the dough

For the Filling

1/2 cup — *Mawa*
1/2 cup — *Powdered sugar*
3 tbsps — *Chopped almond and pistachios*
2 tbsps — *Raisins*
1/4 tsp — *Powdered cardamom*
A pinch of nutmeg
Clarified butter for frying

METHOD

For the filling

Place all the ingredients for the filling in a bowl and mix well. Set aside.

For the dough

Mix clarified butter in the flour and make a semi-soft dough. Set aside for 30 minutes. Divide the dough in 8-10 balls and cover and keep. Roll each one into three inch circles. Take one tablespoon of filling in the centre and apply little water on the edges. Fold over the dough to form half moon shape. Lightly press to seal the edges. You may use the mould to do this or do it by hand. Crimp the edges to give the finish. Repeat for the remaining dough. Heat clarified butter in a wide pan and fry mewavati on a slow flame, three-four at a time until golden. Drain and set aside. Let it cool completely and fill in the airtight container. Use as required.

Note: You can replace mawa with dessicated coconut.

Badam Katli
(Diamond-shaped Almond Sweet)

Makes 30 pieces

INGREDIENTS

2 cups	*Blanched almonds*
¾ cup	*Sugar*
½ tsp	*Cardamom powder*
A few strands of saffron	
2-3	*Thin silver foil sheets*
1 tbsp	*Clarified butter (ghee)*

METHOD

Drop almonds in hot water and let it stand for 10 minutes. Remove from water and peel off the skin. Pat dry. Grind to a fine powder. Place sugar in a thick vessel and add enough water to cover the surface. Place on a high flame to make syrup. Boil till it forms two-three strands. Add cardamom powder and saffron mixed with little water. Add almond powder and continue mixing. When the sugar and almonds have incorporated properly, remove from stove (approximately two-three minutes). Apply clarified butter on the counter or work surface. Turn out the almond mixture on it. Immediately start rolling to the required thickness. Even out the mixture and press silver foil to cover. Cut diagonally for diamond shapes. Let it cool to room temperature. Remove with sharp, flat spoon. Store in an airtight box.

Note : Almonds can be replaced by cashews. Slightly toast the cashews before powdering them.

Mewavati

Badam Katli (centre)

Cashew Puri Sandwich

Traditional Waffles

Traditional Waffles

Makes 8 waffles

INGREDIENTS

4	*Eggs*
2 cups	*Sifted plain flour*
1 tsp	*Salt*
1 tsp	*Baking soda*
1 tsp	*Baking powder*
2 cups	*Buttermilk*
1 cup	*Melted butter*

To Serve

Maple syrup or golden syrup

METHOD

Beat the eggs until light. Sift together flour, salt, soda and baking soda. Add the flour mixture and buttermilk alternately to the beaten eggs, beginning and ending with the flour mixture. Add melted butter; blend thoroughly. Refrigerate until used. Remove from the fridge half an hour before you want to use it. Heat the waffle iron 10 minutes prior to use. For each waffle, pour about half a cup of batter into the centre of the lower half of the waffle iron until it spreads one inch from the edges. Shut the cover gently and cook until the iron stops steaming. Do not raise the cover during baking. Remove and serve immediately with butter and hot maple syrup.

The above traditional recipe is used for different types of flavors. Some of the options I really liked are as follows:

- Heat half a cup of maple syrup and additional melted butter to serve.
- Heat half a cup strawberry puree along with half a cup of sugar, two teaspoons of corn flour and one teaspoon of lemon juice. Bring to a boil until slightly thickened and translucent. Serve warm.
- Mix one teaspoon of powdered cinnamon with half a cup of powdered sugar and sprinkle this onto hot waffles.

Eggless Waffles

Makes 8 Waffles

INGREDIENTS

2 cups	*Plain flour*
½ tsp	*Salt*
1 tsp	*Sugar*
2 tsps	*Baking powder*
1½ tsps	*Soda Bicarbonate*
2 cups	*Thick buttermilk*
6 tbsps	*Melted butter*

To Serve

Golden syrup or Maple syrup

METHOD

Sieve the flour with salt, baking powder, soda and sugar. Mix buttermilk with the butter. Mix wet and dry ingredients alternately little at a time, to make a smooth batter. Cover and keep for half an hour. Heat the waffle iron 10 minutes prior to serving. Apply a little butter on the iron and pour the mixture with a ladle to cover the iron plates. Bake for eight to ten minutes or until light brown. Remove and serve immediately with hot syrup.

Note: For variation, refer to the traditional waffle recipe.

Baci
(Chocolate-Walnut Kisses)

Makes 32 small cups

INGREDIENTS

200 gms	*Walnuts, roasted and finely chopped*
200 gms	*Thick cream*
250 gms	*Dark cooking chocolate*
3-4 tbsps	*Icing sugar*
2 tbsps	*Dark rum*
32	*Small paper cups*

METHOD

Heat the cream in a pan and melt the chocolate, stirring constantly. Once melted and incorporated with cream, remove from heat and add sugar and rum. Chill until just firm. Set three to four tiny pieces of walnuts in each paper cup. Beat the chocolate mixture until smooth and fill the chocolate mixture in a piping bag with a star nozzle. Pipe a swirl of chocolate over the nuts in each cup and chill until firm. They will stay in the fridge for up to one week in an air-tight container.

Chocolate Cups with Strawberry Cream

Makes 12 cups

INGREDIENTS

For the cups

3/4 cup	*Chopped semi-sweet cooking chocolate*
15 gms	*Butter*
8-10 pieces	*Paper cups*

For the Cream

225 gms	*Strawberries, washed and sliced thinly*
2/3 cup	*Thick cream*
2 tbsps	*Icing sugar*

METHOD

For the Cups

Break the chocolate into small pieces and heat with butter over hot water until melted and smooth, stirring occasionally to blend well. Take out eight paper cups for use. Holding each case at an angle, dribble some chocolate into it, one teaspoon at a time, until the whole cup is thinly coated. Repeat with the remaining cups. Chill for about 30 minutes or until set. (You could do this in two batches to avoid thickening of the chocolate). Remove one paper case at a time from the refrigerator and peel off the paper, leaving behind a chocolate cup. Stand the cups on a chilled serving plate until required for further use.

For the Cream

Whip the cream with icing sugar until stiff peaks are formed. Gently fold in the strawberries, reserving some for decoration, and keep cold. Just before serving, fill the cups with the strawberry mixture and decorate with strawberry slices.

Variations for the Fillings

Orange Cream: 100 gms of two tablespoons of fresh cream, two tablespoons of orange liqueur or orange essence, four-five slices of fresh oranges, peeled, four tablespoons of custard.

Cocoa Cream: One-third cup cream plus three tablespoons of icing sugar in which you fold three tablespoons of cocoa powder and half a teaspoon of vanilla essence.

Chocolate Dipped Strawberries

Makes 1 kg

INGREDIENTS

500 gms	*Fresh strawberries*
500 gms	*Plain chocolate, dark and white*

METHOD

Choose ripe, firm, well-coloured strawberries with their stems intact. Wash the strawberries, leaving the stems on and pat them dry. Melt both the chocolates separately over two pans of boiling water. Remove from heat and set aside to cool slightly. Holding each strawberry from the stem, dip half of them into dark chocolate and the other half into white, leaving the top uncovered. Allow the excess chocolate to drip off. Place the strawberries on a tray lined with foil or greaseproof paper and allow them to dry completely. Store in a cool place.

Variation

Crystallized orange peel and crystallized ginger dipped in this way are also delicious.

Cocoa Meringues

Makes 12

INGREDIENTS

2	*Egg whites*
1/4 cup	*Castor sugar*
1/4 cup	*Icing sugar*
2 tsps	*Cocoa powder*

A pinch of cream of tartar

Oil for greasing

For the Filling

1/2 cup	*Whipping cream*
2 tbsps	*Castor sugar*
2 tsps	*Cocoa powder*

A few drops vanilla essence

METHOD

Beat the egg whites in a clean dry bowl until they form stiff peaks. Add castor sugar, little at a time, beating well after each addition. Continue till both the sugars are added and the mixture looks stiff and glossy. Gently fold in the cocoa powder. Spoon the mixture in a piping bag fitted with half an inch star nozzle. Lightly oil a baking sheet and cover it with greaseproof paper and oil the paper as well. Pipe the meringue into spirals, one and a half inches in diameter, onto the baking sheet.

Bake the meringues in a preheated oven at 110° C or 225° F for two-three hours or until meringues are completely dry. Remove them from the baking tray and cool on a wire rack. Store in an airtight jar and alternately sandwich them with chocolate cream.

For the Filling

Whip the cream and sugar in a stainless steel bowl until peaks are formed. Fold in the cocoa powder. Spoon this mixture in a piping bag and swirl the cream at the base of one meringue and sandwich with the other one. Repeat for all the meringues. Arrange them on a serving plate and keep them cold or serve immediately.

Khopra Pak
(Coconut Sweet)

Make approx. 34 pieces

INGREDIENTS

5 cups	*Freshly grated coconut*
½ cup	*Fresh cream from top of milk*
1 ½ cup	*Sugar*
1 cup	*Condensed milk*
½ tsp	*Saffron powder*
1 tsp	*Cardamom powder*
1 tbsp	*Clarified butter*
2 tbsps	*Pistahcio, chopped into pieces*

To Garnish

Rose Petals

METHOD

In a large vessel, mix together coconut and cream and set aside for half an hour. Apply clarified butter to 14" stainless steel or silver plates with a small little high rim. Heat broad aluminum vessel (kadai), add soaked coconut and dry roast it for eight to ten minutes. When the coconut becomes dry, add sugar and condensed milk and mix well. Cook on medium heat for 15-20 minutes. Check with your finger, if it forms a thick syrupy single strand, remove from stove. Add the powdered saffron mixed with a little milk and cardamom powder. Mix well, pour this into the prepared stainless steel plate and smoothen the surface with the back of a spoon. Sprinkle pistachio pieces on top. Let it cool completely. Cut across to make one inch by one inch square or diamond pieces. Remove from the plate with the help of a flat spoon and put it on a serving plate and garnish with rose petals.

Lemon Bars

Makes 30 bars

INGREDIENTS

For the Crust

1 cup	*Plain flour, sieved*
1/4 cup	*Powdered sugar*
1/4 cup	*Butter*

For the Topping

3/4 cup	*Vanilla/caramel chips*
3/4 cup	*Powdered sugar*
2	*Eggs*
1/4 tsp	*Baking powder*
1/4 tsp	*Lemon rind*
1/4 cup	*Lemon juice*
1/4 cup	*Plain flour*
1/4 cup	*Icing sugar*

METHOD

Heat oven to 350°F. In a medium bowl, stir together all the ingredients for the base and press it onto the bottom of nine inches square or 11"x 9"baking pan. Bake for 15 minutes until it turns light brown. Remove from oven and sprinkle vanilla chips over the crust. In a medium bowl, stir together all the ingredients for the topping except the icing sugar. Pour carefully over the chips and crust. Bake for 15 minutes or until set. Cool on a wire rack; Sprinkle with icing sugar. Cool completely and cut into bars.

Glossary

Glossary

HINTS AND TECHNIQUE FOR SUCCESSFUL DESSERTS

1. Read the recipe correctly and make sure all the equipments and ingredients are on hand. Try not to use substitutes.
2. Sift flour or any other dry ingredient before measuring.
3. Use appropriate measuring cups, spoons and glass cups.
4. Use correct size pans, pie dishes, moulds and bowls as mentioned.
5. Always wait for five to seven minutes after removing the dish from the oven before inverting or serving.
6. Any recipe where two different mixtures are to be blended together, always fold in 1/3 first and then the remaining mixture. This way you will retain lightness of the mixture.
7. Adjust oven racks and temperature before hand.
8. For pastries and pies, use as little pressure as possible to assemble the dough and to roll to achieve lighter product.
9. Eggs should be used at room temperature for best results.
10. While whipping the cream, use stainless steel bowl. For best result, make sure the cream is cold and beaten over a bowl of ice.
11. To help prevent any pastry base from getting soggy, brush it lightly with beaten egg white. Refrigerate 15 minutes before baking or filling.
12. Do not over cook chocolate while melting or it will lose the shine. Add a tablespoon of vegetable oil to the chocolate before melting for smooth chocolate.
13. Incorporate stiffly beaten egg whites into base mixture immediately after beating or it will begin to deflate.
14. Separate the eggs while they are cold.
15. Gelatine powder should always be mixed with cold liquid, allow soaking and then heat gently stirring continuously. Strain before using.
16. Cream cheeses should be used in any dessert at room temperature.
17. Plain sponge cakes for puddings should be soaked with sugar syrup mixed with relevant flavours for extra moistness.
18. Frozen dessert containers should be tightly covered with cling wrap or foil before freezing them. Thaw them one-two hours before serving in lower part of the refrigerator.
19. Toast nuts or biscuits in an ungreased baking sheet over medium heat before chopping, slicing or powdering them to give crispier texture.
20. To make lightened whipped cream to serve with desserts, beat one egg white until soft peaks form and fold into two cups of whipped cream.

21. Do as much advanced preparation as possible before you start the cooking. This will save time.
22. When measuring butter, etc. bring it down to room temperature if cold; then press the spoon into the measuring cup and level off.
23. When measuring liquids, use standard glass measuring cup. Always place cup on flat surface and at eye level.
24. While rolling the pastry, keep lifting rolling pin time to time. This helps to keep the pastry light.

EQUIVALENT MEASURES

1 tablespoon = 3 teaspoons

1 tablespoons = ¼ cup

1 fluid ounce = 2 tablespoons

1 ounce = 25 gms

1 ounce = 4 level tablespoons

16 ounces = 1 pound

1 cup = ½ pint (liquid)

2 pints = 1 quart

1 cup = 200 gms

COOKING TERMINOLOGY

Bake: To cook by dry heat in the oven.

Batter: A mixture of flour, liquid and sometimes other ingredients, of a thin, creamy consistency.

Beat: To work a mixture smooth with regular, hard, rhythmic movements.

Brush: To spread food with butter, oil or egg using pastry brush.

Blend: To mix thoroughly two or more ingredients.

Boil: To cook in liquid at a temperature of 100°C or 212°F.

Brule: French word for burnt.

Caramel: Sugar heated to a rich brown coloured syrup.

Chill: To cool food without freezing, in a refrigerator.

Flambé: A dish flavoured with flamed alcohol. Usually brandy or sherry ignited and allowed to burn either on finished dish or in the pan during cooking.

Fold in: To combine a light, whisked or creamed mixture with other ingredients so that it retains its lightness.

Garnish: Edible decoration added to any dish to improve the appearance.

Melt: To heat solid food like sugar, butter, until it becomes liquid.

Parfait: A light, cream enriched, iced dessert, often with fruit puree.

Toss: To mix foods lightly with a lifting motion, using two spoons or forks.

Whip: To rapidly beat in order to incorporate air and expand volume.